The Gift of Birth

Dedicated to my children: Ben, Maria, Julia, Alex, and Matthew.
—Susan Windley-Daoust

Susan Windley-Daoust

The Gift of Birth

Discerning God's Presence During Childbirth

Our Sunday Visitor
www.osv.com

Nihil obstat: Rev. Timothy Hall
Censor deputatus
December 12, 2015

Imprimatur: †Most Rev. John M. Quinn
Bishop of Winona
December 12, 2015

The *imprimatur* is an official declaration that a book or pamphlet is free of doctrinal or moral error. No implication is contained therein that those who have granted the imprimatur agree with the contents, opinions, or statements expressed.

Cover and book design and build by Steve Nagel. Cover art © 2019, 2015 by Owen Swain. Discover more art by Owen at owenswain.com. Copyediting by Nancee Adams-Taylor.

24 23 22 21 20 19   2 3 4 5 6 7 8 9

ISBN: 978-1-68192-521-9 (Inventory No. T2410)
LCCN: 2019939968

PRINTED IN THE UNITED STATES OF AMERICA

Contents

Foreword: The Spiritual Meaning of Childbirth 7

The Theology of the Body and Childbirth

1. You Are Called: What Is the Call to Motherhood? 21
2. The Law of the Gift: A Brief Introduction to the Theology of the Body 27
3. Take, Lord, Receive: The Spiritual Nature of Giving and Receiving 32
4. "Lord, Teach Me to See": How Do We See the Holy Spirit in Giving Birth? 37
5. Wait—Isn't Birth Supposed to Hurt? 41
6. Your Spiritual Keys in the Process of Giving Birth: Relax, Cooperate, and Yield to God 46

Reading the Signs of Birth

7. Choosing Wonder: The Conception of a Child 51
8. Waiting: "How Long, O Lord?" 59
9. Opening: First Contractions 64
10. Focusing on Love: Active Labor 71
11. Yielding to the Work of the Holy Spirit 77
12. Trusting: The Transition from Contractions to Pushing 82
13. Cooperating with God: Pushing and Letting Birth Happen 88
14. Receiving the Child 93
15. Last Thoughts on Giving Birth 99

When Childbearing Is Difficult, Where Is God?

16. Difficulty Conceiving: He Heals the Brokenhearted 102

17. The Unexpected Child: Dealing with Shock, Fear, and Anxiety 107

18. Miscarriage and Stillbirth: Grieving the Child Who Goes with God 112

19. A High-Risk Birth: Are Medical Interventions Clouding the Sign of Birth? 118

20. Postpartum Depression: When Contentment Cannot Be Felt 122

Seeking the Holy Spirit in Birth Stories

21. JoAnna: "God Was Present Throughout" 128

22. Carla: "I'm Going to Feel This Birth" 132

23. Leah: "God Is All Over Body and Birth for Me" 137

24. Karen: "I Remember Praying Through the Pain in a New Way" 141

25. Kendra: "I Feel Closer to God in My Weakness" 147

26. Regina: "After the C-Sections, I See the Hand of God in All Things" 151

27. Jennifer: "Mary Became My Lifeline" 154

28. Nora: "I Kept Thinking, 'This Is My Body, Given Up for You'" 159

Notes 164

Acknowledgments 171

Foreword

The Spiritual Meaning of Childbirth

> . . . if I were to name my own most profound spiritual or theological experience, without hesitation I would cite the birth of my three children. This has nothing to do with my fondness for babies as such—like everyone else they can be charming or difficult, attractive or not—nor with my personal (and biased) relationship with my own children. Rather, each birth was a glimpse into the mystery of Creation and Incarnation.[1]

> When we had our first child, admittedly a somewhat easy delivery with no medicine involved, I felt as though my husband and I were with God at the dawn of creation. Nothing . . . brought me as close to a sense of God creating and loving his creation ("And God saw that it was good") as that morning when the air was as pure as the day after a storm and God's power and love flooded the room. It remains, along with the delivery of my second child, the most deeply spiritual experience of my life.[2]

> [W]orking with the delivery process . . . can be a growing personal, emotional, mental, physical, and spiritual experience. But we have to take the chance and work through the experience. By my fourth delivery, [which occurred] on Holy Saturday, I had a mystical experience that I wouldn't trade for any pain-free, medically induced delivery. While I know we are all different and have different pain thresholds, I always viewed myself as weak when it came to pain, but through each childbirth God showed me how strong I can be when I unite myself to Him. With Him I can accomplish anything that is within His will.[3]

How often have we heard this—a woman identifying giving birth to her child as one of her deepest spiritual experiences? Her husband, the child's father, often responds that way as well, with a speechless awe after the baby is born.

Yet it is hard to talk about. It's so much easier to talk about the "brass tacks" medical details: epidurals and dilation and birthing positions and the pros and cons of water birth. It's true that women may often speak easily of the spiritual gift that is their newborn child. But what about the *experience* of giving birth to that child? If giving birth can be a spiritual experience, why do we never explore how that is so? Is there something designed by God in the process of giving birth that leads us to experience the presence of God in a profound way?

I am a mother to five children, four born to me and the fifth adopted into our family. After the first three births—all of which "spoke" to me in different ways—my life went down a new road. I experienced a renewal of my life in Christ that was by equal measures unexpected and soul shaking, and it led me to a deep appreciation of birth as a model of the spiritual life, and a spiritual experience in itself. Allow me to share a personal story that might shed some light on what I mean:

> When my third child was one year old, I experienced a few weeks of unsettled discontent with my by-all-external-accounts flourishing life—sadness, emptiness, and scattershot anxiety about everything and nothing. One night I had a dream about going to confession. In the dream, I approached the confessional door, but didn't step inside. This dream played on repeat all night long. I woke up rattled and wondering what the dream could mean. Amid my wondering, I decided to attend daily Mass. The homily had nothing to do with the Scripture readings for the day, focusing instead on the virtues of going to confession. Truly unnerved by this point, I walked back to my office and promptly made an appointment with my

> pastor to hear my confession. The next day, I was "living the dream," standing outside the confessional and wondering what on Earth I was doing there. Suddenly, it occurred to me: I had not been praying. Granted, the anxiety I had been experiencing made it hard—but I had also given up. That is what I needed to confess. So, I did.
>
> Later that evening, I began to pray, and was overwhelmed by an experience of the Holy Spirit. Where there was once nothing (or so it felt), suddenly there was SOMETHING, infinitely more than I could handle. It was beautiful, but also scary. I didn't know what was going on, really, but I knew I was not in control of what was happening, and was unsure why God wanted to give me such joy (there was that) but also such pain, such literally painful homesickness. A strangely familiar and unfamiliar joy and pain and life and dying that pointed me to God, and said "Pay attention."

The reason I share this? As I moved into the intensely God-breathed days that followed this experience, a single clarifying thought kept returning to me: *This is a lot like giving birth; it feels as if something is trying to be born.* And it did, in my soul and in the marrow of my bones: impossible to distract oneself away from this, a sudden clearing in the forest of life, an expectant and somewhat painful waiting, a knowing what to do and not knowing what to do all at once, the sense that my life is changing here and now. I remembered, with surprise and gratitude: *I've been here before.* Spiritually, this reminded me intensely, startlingly, of when I gave birth. And that experience of giving birth gave me a sense of how to handle the gift of prayer that God so graciously gave me.

Since human beings are a unity of body and soul, this shouldn't be that surprising. The spirit affects the body, and the body the spirit, in mysterious ways.[4] To anyone who thinks that something as earthy as childbirth cannot have a spiritual dimension, I ask, how could it not? Especially since it is not some random bodily function, but part of the first covenant God made with Adam and Eve to be fruitful? True, childbirth is part of the fallen world, and I will talk about that. But it doesn't lose its design to point the mother and those helping her to the lavish love of God. Childbirth has a spiritual meaning that goes beyond the existence of new life—as profound as that is. *Childbirth teaches us how to make room for God, receive grace, and live in relationship with the Holy Spirit.*

Spiritual direction: Paying attention to God's work in your birthing

This book of reflections is meant to help you to see, pray, and reflect upon the process of giving birth.

This is not a theology textbook as much as a book based in spiritual direction. Spiritual direction is an ancient practice in the Christian tradition, beginning with the third century desert hermits who provided guidance to seekers of wisdom. It evolved into a relationship where two people, a "director" and a "directee," both disciples on the way, sift through everyday experiences of prayer and relationship, and work to find the movement of the Holy Spirit. The Holy Spirit is the true director of human souls, and spiritual direction is used by many as a help to better pay attention to the Spirit and grow in depth, love, and holiness.

I am drawing on two saints in these reflections. Firstly, St. Ignatius of Loyola. St. Ignatius (1491–1556) is widely recognized as the Father of modern spiritual direction. I suggest using his method of "imaginative prayer" in some of the "For Prayerful Reflection" pieces. Ignatius is also the source of the grounding insight of this book, the "First Foundation"—recognizing that everything is a gift from God meant to lead us to God—as well as the imperative to prefer nothing over Christ.

Secondly, an undeniable influence is a new saint, Pope St. John Paul II. John Paul II wrote and delivered a series of audiences, or short oral presentations, commonly dubbed the Theology of the Body. If you are not familiar with the Theology of the Body, there are many popular treatments on the subject.[5] The importance of the Theology of the Body for this topic is that John Paul II says explicitly the body and its covenantal relationships have meaning; that they are created as signs that point to God. We can, and should, learn to "read the language of the body." It is these insights—combined with the deep Carmelite spiritual roots planted in those audiences—that encourage us to explore those signs of birth as a way God communicates with us, not just mechanical accidents of nature.

There is a rich tradition within spiritual direction being brought to bear here. But neither of these saints (nor I) can tell you what to feel or experience. We want to help you pay attention to where the Holy Spirit may be a more visible and felt presence in the birth of your child. Only you, with the essential help of the Holy Spirit, can discover and recognize the Holy Spirit acting in your life. We can affirm, encourage, and perhaps challenge what you see. And I am encouraging you to lean on Christian spiritual wisdom in the practical realities of giving birth. But in the end, this set of reflections should fade to the background, and the holy conversation should exist not between you and a book, but between you and God.

Your body is not a machine: Re-reading the language of the body

One of the insights held by our "patron saints" is that it is challenging, in a fallen world, to see rightly. Sin has an effect on our ability to see the human being as a unity of body and soul.[6]

Much of the Theology of the Body argues that we are inspired to protect the goodness of the body by veiling it from the fallen sight. This isn't a wrong move—it is more a protective move, and an acknowledgment that the body is of value and worth preserving. But it does indicate that after the Fall, something changed with *the way we perceive* the other. The fallen sight that John Paul II talks about most directly is lust: and in the context of Adam and Eve, sexuality and marriage, that makes sense. But there is another fallen sight at play, and one that skews the vision we have of childbirth—the fallen sight of materialism. We treat the body apart from the soul. We increasingly see the body as a machine, perhaps a beautiful one, but one we can name and manipulate and control. We lose the sense of the body as a sign to be read, the form of the soul, and see it instead as an instrument to be used. We lose the heart of what it means to be human, a unity of body and soul. For this fallen sight as well, we need to take to heart John Paul II's admonition to "reread the language of the body."

In the Western world, we have made great strides in making sure pregnant women have access to medical attention through prenatal care. But women about to give birth, and women who have given birth, are in deep need of *spiritual* attention as well. Our standard medical protocols place any spiritual understanding of childbirth as a side interest at best, and an undermining foe at worst. I do not mean to scorn the science, nor many dedicated and caring medical professionals. There are indeed many excellent doctors and midwives, and we thank God for many advances in helping those with high-risk pregnancies, and helping sick children survive and thrive in ways unimaginable decades ago. But I will not mince words: any spiritual "rereading" of the process of childbirth is under attack, and we do not know how to respond to this spiritual battle. In fact, we barely recognize what is being lost.

Let me again give a brief example from my own life, my

first childbirth, to illustrate what happens when the person is treated like an object. The birth began with a few challenges, but deteriorated at the halfway point:

> My first child was born through an unnecessarily difficult birth. I was healthy, he was healthy, and the only medical concern was that he was taking his sweet time to be born: forty-seven hours. My water broke in the middle of the night and I had a very slow twenty hours of puttering contractions at home. We went in to the hospital in the middle of the second night of labor to find out I was only at 3 cm dilated.
>
> In the next twenty-seven hours I slept a couple of hours, walked all over that hospital about fifty times, was refused food or water other than a few sips of Sprite, and kept having bizarre conversations with my assigned midwife, a woman I met that morning who had passive-aggression down to an art form. I questioned whether the length of the labor, and certain events within it, indicated something was wrong, but she argued back, "Honey, this is what natural childbirth feels like!" (Later, it was determined my son's positioning was really poor for a natural birth: he was posterior asynclitic, which meant facing the wrong direction and with an extreme head tilt. This painful position could have been adjusted, or at least diagnosed—but I had no idea at the time.) Finally, after a shot of Nubain (or the intensity of the situation) caused me to blank out for a couple of hours, I was at full dilation; but by then, I was too exhausted to push. Not just tired—exhausted. I couldn't move any muscles if my life depended on it. I actually slept (or passed out) for nearly five hours after active labor, through the pushing contractions. I ended up giving birth through a Cesarean section for "failure to progress." My baby was born in the middle of the night in an operating room while I was strapped down and numbed, my husband dressed like he was ready to step onto a *Grey's Anatomy* set.

My son was pulled from my womb, cried vigorously, and was found healthy. I was grateful. But I was also a physical, emotional, and spiritual mess.

Now, if it were simply a matter of mistakes, pain, bad luck, and facing the unwanted C-section, the birthing process would have been difficult to accept, but spiritually neutral. I am leery of calling everything unfortunate a "spiritual attack." But there was more than unfortunate surgery going on: the way I (and my son, and my husband) were treated in the long "interventions phase" (*a.k.a.* active labor) was spiritually damaging. Consistently, I was treated like an object—and a problematic object at that—one that didn't want the epidural and was taking forever to give birth! They were "doing birth" to me rather than helping me "give birth." I was surprised by this, since I had chosen the hospital based on the availability of midwives, who tend to be very sympathetic to letting the birthing mother and child lead. The passive-aggressive midwife in particular was a genius at treating me like an object, flippantly dismissing what turned out to be legitimate concerns, laughing (really) at my pain, mocking my ongoing attempt to give birth without drugs, and strapping me into a mind-bogglingly agonizing position and walking away for an hour. I cannot overstate how strange those particular twelve hours were. She really treated me like she hated me, but with a smile.[7] That birth experience ended up being spiritually abusive by the ongoing treatment of me as an object (and not just an object; close to an object of ridicule). And my experience may have been worse than some, but it was not that unusual. Any treatment of laboring women and their soon-to-be-born children as objects and products opens the door to spiritual warfare. By denying the humanity in the room, the battle is already on.

There is need for healing—so many women need healing from childbirth experiences where they were spiritually abused and objectified. But there is also a need for truth. The culturally accepted canard that "childbirth will break you—you can't do it without the drugs, that's just life and it needs to be this way" is a lie. And lies, at their root, come from the father of lies.[8] They are to be identified and rejected. Sometimes birth is incredibly difficult, yes, and when things are going wrong, medical interventions are right and good. We thank God for them! But a typical birth doesn't have to be undoable and destructive—that is simply not normal. Women's bodies and souls were created by God to be able to do this very thing: to give birth. And God is *always present.* The act of giving birth can be a teaching moment in the spiritual life, and a moment of grace. The dignity of birthing emphatically needs to be spoken to in spiritual ways.

If there is a silver lining to having a difficult first birth experience, it is that I became extremely intentional and attentive to my next three birth experiences:

- My second labor and delivery was still on the long side, twenty-six hours, but much simpler and a beautiful experience, supported by midwives, a doula,[9] and my husband. Even though my daughter's birth was complicated by a compound presentation[10] and I needed surgery immediately after that natural VBAC (vaginal birth after Cesarean), it was a powerfully moving experience. I remember no really significant pain—just intensity.
- My third birth was concentrated. This daughter decided, after a puttering-all-day labor, that she was going to barrel out like she was on the autobahn. She was also born through a natural VBAC, although when things kicked into high gear, I turned to my husband and our doula and said, "You know how I have always said I'm not doing an epidural? I need an epidural. Now." But by the time we got to the hospital, there was no time for it—it was practically time to push. She was the first child I could hold and cuddle for an hour right after the birth.

- My fourth birth was the shortest labor of the bunch, thirteen hours (I'm a slow laborer: the average labor is about eight hours), the first one where I wanted to throw up at some point, and also somewhat rushed toward the end. His birth was a bit different in that the pushing was hard (he was a huge baby), and there was some concern about getting him out more quickly. But he was fine in the end, and so was I. His birth was also a natural VBAC.

- Our fifth child was welcomed into our family through adoption. He was five years old when we adopted him, and the size of a two-year-old, with significant medical issues. Many people asked at the time which was harder, giving birth or doing the waiting and paperwork of adoption. (In our case, both were nine months long.) Obviously it depends, but the adoption was no picnic. The waiting, concern, and worry were more intense with this son, because we knew he needed medical help available in the United States as soon as possible. And we knew that adopting him was only the beginning of helping him to recover from a poor start in life and to attach to our family. We knew there were no guarantees it would be smooth sailing. My hat is tipped to any other parent who goes through the adoption process; it isn't easy. But it can be very much worth it. We love this son deeply, and so do our other children.

The focus of this book, though, is to honor the dignity of childbirth by recovering "the language of the body," as John Paul II puts it. A woman's body was created to give birth—and while she may be called by God to do so or not, that sign is important. Through interviews with other women and my own experience, I hope to share a vision of how to be open to the call to give birth, and the dignity of the experience.

You will notice that I focus first on the signs present in a natural childbirth. I realize many people in the United States medically supplement their childbirths, and sometimes, birth *needs* to be augmented for the health of the mother and baby. But natural childbirth is closer to what God originally created. Augmentation may be necessary in our fallen reality, and we can thank God it is available to help women and their children as much as possible complete a healthy birth. But it is part of our now imperfect and fallen world. As we look for signs of God's presence in birth, I will present the signs you see in natural childbirth as offering a clearer vision of how the birth process points us to God. However, I also will present how people giving birth in a more medically supplemented manner can adjust these insights to their situation. Ultimately, the type of childbirth you have is a decision between you, your doctor, and God. And the Holy Spirit is present and active at every single birth, augmented or not.

How do I use this book?

This book is meant to be read as a way to spiritually prepare for giving and receiving birth. Perhaps you could use it as a weekly set of reflections to consider before you give birth, a kind of devotional reading. And for those who have given birth, my hope is that these reflections may help you remember and spiritually process your previous experiences of birth. After all, time stands still in the heart of God. You can return to that time in prayer, either in gratitude or to ask for healing.

I personally encourage you to use Christian spirituality as a preparation for your birth. There is a sad lack of Christian-specific materials out there, and I hope this book will fill a gap. But our Christian faith abundantly addresses and fills every aspect of human existence. Even if you come across other "helps," don't be tempted to treat your birth as a New Age experience. The Holy Trinity defines our lives, and all riches are found therein.

This book in no way substitutes for a childbirth

preparation class. Please, do the research necessary to make informed and wise choices for a birth plan, a medical professional, a hospital, and so on. Personally, I have found William Sears, M.D., and Martha Sears, R.N.'s book *The Birth Book: Everything You Need to Know to Have a Satisfying Birth* both informative and evenhanded.[11] They do advocate for the medical advantages of an unmedicated childbirth, but are aware that medical intervention can be important and life-saving in a variety of circumstances, and offer advice on how to consider those options. The book is accessible, has medical heft, and is peppered with a wide variety of birth stories. I highly recommend it.

The structure of this book

The first part of the book is a series of reflections on how the birthing body serves as a sign, and how birthing has its own "language." If you are not familiar with the Theology of the Body, this is where I introduce it and make connections between Pope St. John Paul II's insights and receiving life as a gift . . . which includes the process of giving birth. This section also addresses what is confusing for many Christians: how birth can be a *gift* when we read in Genesis 3:16, "To the woman he said, 'I will greatly increase your pangs in childbearing; in pain you shall bring forth children, yet your desire shall be for your husband, and he shall rule over you.'"

The second part of the book reflects on how prominent physical and emotional signs in the process of giving birth "speak" to us spiritually. How can these experiences naturally lead us to openness to the Holy Spirit? How can we approach these stages remembering that the Holy Spirit is "the Lord and Giver of Life"?

The third section of the book ponders what happens when things do not go according to plan. What if you cannot get pregnant? What if you miscarry? Or you anticipate a high-risk birth? What if you develop postpartum depression? These situations all require you to lean on the Holy Spirit as Comforter, Advocate, and Guide in new, but hopefully familiar ways.

Finally, the book ends with birth stories and interviews with Catholic mothers. Every story is different and every story bears the mark of the Holy Spirit. The wide variety of these childbirth experiences is offered to help you see the infinite creativity of the Holy Spirit's action in the birth of a child—and in the key moment of accepting the vocation to motherhood.

As I will highlight later, your spiritual keys in this process are to be open to receiving what God is doing in the moment, to cooperate with God's intention to realize your motherhood through your body now, and to yield to the work of the Holy Spirit. In short: relax, cooperate, and yield to God. This requires real trust, but God is absolutely trustworthy. My prayer is that you find this set of reflections, wherever you are on your birth journey, helpful in seeing more clearly the amazing midwifery of the Holy Spirit.

The Theology of the Body and Childbirth

1

You Are Called: What Is the Call to Motherhood?

> The couple approached me after the service, and her husband proudly announced to me that they were expecting their first child; his wife was three months pregnant. I congratulated them both, and as the husband moved on to tell other friends, I asked his wife sympathetically how she was feeling. I expected her to speak of morning sickness and tiredness. Instead, she looked at me in quiet awe. "I don't know what I did to deserve such happiness," she said shyly, softly. "How is it that God has chosen me to hold and bear, in my very body, this kind of love?"[12]

Indeed, how is it that God has chosen me? It is a reality well worth pondering—like Mary, the Mother of God, did—in your heart.

We are all chosen, according to the Lord. "You did not choose me but I chose you. And I appointed you to go and bear fruit, fruit that will last, so that the Father will give you whatever you ask him in my name" (John 15:16). We are all called to different vocations: priest, consecrated life, marriage, or the faithful single life. And some of us are also called to physically "bear fruit" through motherhood.

But what does it mean to be called to motherhood? It's hard to know, exactly: yes, it is something you do, but even more so, it is someone you are. And if you are a woman in the Western world, it can be hard to know who you are.

You may know your name, your background, your hobbies, and your talents. But it is harder to know *who you are before God.*

Let me put it this way: Why do companies spend billions of dollars every year on advertisements urging women to embrace some definition of who they are? These advertisers capitalize on your uncertainty. Apparently, they say, you are not beautiful enough, not strong enough, not sexy enough, not smart enough, not happy enough. But they will sell you something that will "fix" that—makeup, a diet program, an exercise routine, revealing clothes, snazzy hipster glasses—and if none of that works, aromatherapy. In the end we look good, smell like lavender, and still don't know who we are.

The issues are even more challenging when we narrow the target to motherhood. What does it mean to be a mother? Will a lovingly decorated nursery help? Books? The right educational toys? A plush stroller? A color-coordinated car seat?

I raise all these shopping possibilities not because they are bad in themselves, but because they can distract us from what it really means to be a woman, and to be a mother. Woman is created good: a woman "for her own sake,"[13] an unrepeatable expression of God's goodness, bearing his image. Yet what we hear is often anything but that insight. What we hear is "you don't measure up, and you need to be fixed."

How do we understand who God calls us to be? As a human, as a woman, and possibly, as a mother?

The challenge of "the feminine mystery"

John Paul II attempted to answer the broader question of what it means to be human through a series of addresses given at papal audiences between 1979 and 1984, popularly called the Theology of the Body. George Weigel famously described the Theology of the Body addresses as "a kind of theological time bomb set to go off, with dramatic consequences, sometime in the third millennium of the Church."[14] We'll take a closer look at the Theology of the Body in the next chapter.

Within the Theology of the Body audiences, John Paul II attempts to address the more specific question of what it means to be a woman by using terms such as the "feminine mystery" or the "feminine genius." People respond to this language either with great fascination or great frustration. I'm convinced that those in the latter group are usually shadow-boxing with their own histories, and not reading what he is trying to say. So let's begin with what John Paul II is *not* saying when he states that the feminine mystery helps us understand who a woman called to motherhood was created to be.

The "feminine mystery" does not refer to a Victorian stereotype of the woman. When the pope uses the term *feminine*, he is certainly not referring to negative characteristics like practiced weakness, learned shyness, or "the vapors." He isn't even referring to the entirely neutral preferences some women have for pastels, lace, quiet voices, Pinterest, or home decorating. All those things are perfectly fine if you like them, but they don't define the feminine. Instead, the "feminine mystery" is referring to the way woman was created by God, fully human, as a person who finds herself—she knew herself, she gave of herself, she discovers herself again—in a reciprocal gift of self with the man Adam. She knows herself in relationship, first and foremost, to God. This is most manifest, the pope said, in the motherhood of Eve.

> Already now, we should observe that in Genesis 4:1 the mystery of femininity manifests and reveals itself in its full depth through motherhood, as the text says, "who conceived and gave birth." The woman stands before the man as mother, subject of the new human life that is conceived and develops in her and is born from her into the world. In this way, what also reveals itself is the mystery of the man's

> masculinity, that is, the generative and "paternal" meaning of his body.[15]

And a few paragraphs later, the pope continues:

> The first woman to give birth has full awareness of the mystery of creation, which renews itself in human generation. She also has *full awareness of the creative participation God has in human generation*, his work and that of her husband, because she says, "I acquired a man from the Lord."[16]

Honestly, I am one of the (many) women who have a squeamish reaction to the word *feminine*, unconsciously importing all kinds of frippery with the word. But understanding myself as created for relationship, for love, for God? I can eagerly embrace that. Perhaps those of us uncomfortable with *feminine* can find a different word. Would *womanly* be a better word? *Motherly*? *Marian*? The plethora of possible terms suggests that what we are pointing to is a mystery that is only fleetingly captured by words.

Whichever word you use, remember that you are called. And if there is an uneasiness or emptiness seeking to be filled, take that to God, not the closest store. You cannot buy your way into knowing who you are. Only God's call can give you that identity. To be woman is to recognize that you are created by God as valuable in yourself, with the capacity to give yourself and find yourself in relationship: to God, to husband, to children.

Femininity is discovered, not learned

We are exploring that set of relationships—woman to husband, woman to child, woman to God—through a deep, spiritual gaze at the process of giving birth.

The reflections of the following chapters are meant to

encourage you to lift your life to God and discover what the Holy Spirit is doing in you and through you. Giving birth is not only physical, it is spiritual work. No matter what the culture throws at us as women, the Holy Spirit is the Lord and Giver of Life, and mothers participate in His work. Conception, gestation, and giving birth puts us in the midst of the mystery of creation. There is a reason people through the ages have named the birth of a child as one of the most meaningful spiritual events in their lives. This book, with the assistance of John Paul II's Theology of the Body, is meant to help you read the language of the ensouled pregnant body. It is meant to help you see and understand the dynamic of the gift, and how we have been called to grow into God's love through participation in the gift of life.

John Paul II says "we should observe that in Gen 4:1 the mystery of femininity manifests and reveals itself in its full depth through motherhood, as the text says, 'who conceived and gave birth.'"[17] In the midst of our cooperation with the work of the Holy Spirit, we can gain so very much: we encounter the Holy Spirit, we receive a call (motherhood), we grow in relationship with our husband, and we gain a new person to love. To be sure, there is sacrifice as well. There is nothing "dainty" about childbirth. And as the experience of childbirth has been affected by the Fall, there is a challenge in seeing its design for making manifest God's Spirit and the reception of grace. All of that is held in the mystery of womanhood: the joy, the receiving, the suffering, the gift.

To be clear, to not give birth does *not* make any female less of a woman or less feminine. There are other ways women express that mystery of womanhood. But the process of giving birth is no physical accident that you must soldier through for the sake of a baby. Perhaps it was created as a gift. Perhaps it is an opportunity to grow in our relationship to God. Perhaps it is the space where you will hear and respond to God's call for your life. It is always space where you stand before and with the Holy Spirit, the Giver of Life.

For prayerful reflection

1. Who is the Holy Spirit to you? Look at the section in the *Catechism of the Catholic Church* (§§ 687–747) on the Holy Spirit. (You can find the *Catechism* online.) Are there lines that resonate? Write them down and keep them by your bedside for spiritual reading.

2. Have you ever thought of motherhood as a call from God? Examine your emotions around that idea. If you sense resistance, do you think your understanding of motherhood is flawed, a cultural stereotype? Or are you scared (many people are scared of calls!)? Bring it to God in prayer and ask for peace and clarity.

3. If you are pregnant, or have recently given birth, take this Scripture to prayer:

> The angel said to her, "Do not be afraid, Mary, for you have found favor with God. And now, you will conceive in your womb and bear a son, and you will name him Jesus" (Luke 1:30–31).
>
> . . . Mary treasured all these words and pondered them in her heart (Luke 2:19).

Consider what this annunciation sounds like if you replace Mary's name with your own: *Do not be afraid, ____, for you have found favor with God. And now, you will conceive in your womb and bear a child. . . .* How does this message move you? How do you respond to the angel? How are you led to ponder this experience in your heart?

2

The Law of the Gift: A Brief Introduction to the Theology of the Body

> God's plan and its renewal by Christ, the redeemer, is imprinted deeply within the bodily nature of the person as a pre-given language of self-giving and fruitfulness.[18]

Your body is spiritually meaningful

When I ask my college theology students how to define the body, inevitably someone will say "a vessel." And that understanding has a history in the Western tradition. But the Theology of the Body argues that this understanding of the body is fundamentally wrong: vessels, after all, are decorative, inanimate containers for "what really matters." By contrast, Christian theology has argued throughout its history that we human beings live as a unity of body and soul. Of course, the soul "really matters." But the soul is expressed through the body—*which also matters*. You are not an angel, an all-spiritual being, but incarnate, a human person—and your body was created by God to be spiritually meaningful.

But meaningful in what way? There are two primary themes and insights in the Theology of the Body that speak to that meaning. First, the body was created with a *spousal* meaning. Second, the body was created by God as a *sign*.

To say that the body has a spousal meaning is to say that we were created for intimate relationship: not just friendship, not a casual acquaintance, but an exclusive relationship that involves a "sincere gift of oneself."[19] If we go back to Scripture and God's original intention, we see this clearly: Adam and Eve were designed in similarity and in difference ("This at last is bone of my bones and flesh of my flesh") (Genesis 2:23) for a relationship of reciprocal self-gift that ends in "Be fruitful and multiply" (Genesis 1:28).

It didn't have to be this way, you know. If God wanted the universe to teem with life, he could have created human beings to reproduce through binary fission, like bacteria: "Let's all split in half!" Or by pressing a button. Or by waiting for storks to bring babies from . . . somewhere. But instead, nearly all earthly procreation involves the intimate union of two beings, male and female, who are similar but different, uniting and bringing forth life. Love is designed to unify and to bear fruit.

Love is also designed to operate according to what many call "the Law of the Gift."

The way in which we were created as women and men is meant to serve as a sign that points toward our destiny—union with God. God wants us to be in relationship, and we are created to thrive in relationship. We know that although we are created whole—created good, a unity of body and soul—we are also lacking the fullness of relationship. We thrive in loving relationship, and that love is crowned in fruitfulness.

All of this John Paul II calls "reading the language of the body." It is a beautiful thing: before humanity had the revelation from God that we call Scripture, before we had the witness of the covenant with the nation of Israel, before we had the witness of the Church, we had the primordial language of the body. The ensouled body senses a lack that is ultimately fulfilled in God. The "spousal meaning of the body" refers to a desire for union and exclusive covenant with another. Even the most remote person without exposure to the Christian message bears in his or her body this sign, desires more, and senses that intimate relationship with the Creator brings new life.

This is the Law of the Gift, that we become most fully ourselves in covenantal relationships through the dynamic of giving and receiving.

All things are given to draw us to God

Although the Theology of the Body offers a new language for understanding the ensouled body as a sign that points to God, the idea that we are called to give and receive is not new. St. Ignatius of Loyola, the founder of the Society of Jesus, wrote a famous set of retreat instructions called the Spiritual Exercises. The Exercises open with this passage, known as the First Principle and Foundation (or simply "the First Foundation"):

> The goal of our life is to live with God forever.
> God, who loves us, gave us life.
> Our own response of love allows God's life to flow into us without limit.
>
> All the things in this world are gifts of God,
> presented to us so that we can know God more easily and make a return of love more readily.
>
> As a result, we appreciate and use all these gifts of God insofar as they help us develop as loving persons.
> But if any of these gifts become the center of our lives, they displace God and so hinder our growth toward our goal.
> In everyday life, then, we must hold ourselves in balance before all of these created gifts insofar as we have a choice and are not bound by some obligation.
> We should not fix our desires on health or sickness,
> wealth or poverty, success or failure, a long life or short one.
> For everything has the potential of calling forth in us
> a deeper response to our life in God.
> Our only desire and our one choice should be this:

I want and I choose what better
leads to the deepening of God's life in me.[20]

This is a bracing opening, written by a man who is essentially saying: Today, reader, you face God. Everything that comes your way—that is given to you—can and will lead you to God. Everything is God's gift to us. Take, receive, and see how what is given calls forth a deeper response to our life in God.

I include the First Foundation here because birth is one of God's gifts to you. How you respond to the challenge of birth can deepen God's life in you. The Theology of the Body implies that giving birth was *designed* to deepen God's life in you.

Giving birth is a gift, no matter whether you "achieve" what you think is a picture-perfect birth or not. Most women have challenging but medically uncomplicated childbirths. Others require significant medical intervention. Some are easy, others are hard. The deepening of God's life in you does not occur if you get an A+ on the Childbirth 101 exam. The deepening of God's life in you occurs when you deliberately open yourself to the work of the Holy Spirit in the process of giving birth, no matter what the birth ends up looking like.

All sorts of signs in childbirth may draw you to God. We will try to "read the language" found in the stages of childbirth. But first, let's reflect on what it means to be open to God.

For prayerful reflection:

Reread Ignatius's First Foundation (above).

1. Are there any gifts that have become the center of your life, displacing God?
2. Are there realities in your life that you have not seen as a gift from God, but that could lead you to God?

3. Can you pray that this pregnancy, however difficult or easy it may be, will lead you closer to the heart of God? Write that prayer here, if you choose.

3

Take, Lord, Receive: The Spiritual Nature of Giving and Receiving

> To pray means to open your hands before God. It means slowly relaxing the tension which squeezes your hands together and accepting your existence with an increasing readiness, not as a possession to defend, but as a gift to receive.[21]

So much of being in relationship—to each other, and to God—is about giving and receiving. The more intimate the relationship, the more deeply we give and receive.

Henri Nouwen, a priest and spiritual master of the past century, wrote a small picture book called *With Open Hands*. It is worth finding and reading prayerfully. Nouwen says that we can see our relationship to God through our hands: When we approach God in our minds, in our prayer, do we come with open hands? Or are our hands closed, clenched, hidden, and maybe even ready to strike? If they are closed, how could you possibly receive any gift God wants to give you? If God wants to take your hand in friendship, how could he do it? If you wanted to give someone anything, how could you do it with clenched hands?

But look at open hands. They are relaxed, comfortable, unprotected, a bit vulnerable. They are waiting. You could form them into an offered embrace. You can share what you have. You can form them into a begging bowl. You can receive and you can give with such hands. These open hands are open to relationship. And this should be our spiritual disposition as Christians: we should remember to be in relationship to God with open hands, ready to give and to receive.

How we are created for giving and receiving

When the Theology of the Body says that the ensouled body has a spousal meaning, it means that as men and women we are created to give and receive. And this goes beyond our hands (although how we hold our hands is an important reminder): we are designed to give and receive love in the most intimate of ways. John Paul II offered that women were created with an essential femininity that is receptive, and men were created with an essential masculinity that is generative. In practice, and especially in a well-lived marital covenant, this giving and receiving is mutual and reciprocal.[22] But to stay with women: part of the spousal meaning of our bodies is that we were created with an ability to receive. When a woman receives the love of a man through the conjugal act of intercourse, she opens herself to the designed consequences of that mutual self-gift, one of which may be the gift of new life.

Jesus Christ: "Into your hands . . ."

If you are thinking, "Well, that sounds very poetic, but I'm not sure how love-filled giving and receiving is a sign, or a meaning of the body, or anything beyond my love for my spouse," I have news for you: the Law of the Gift is the very language of Christianity. And we see the most dramatic example of it on Good Friday: when Jesus Christ *gives* his life on a cross, *to* the Father, *for* our sake, *out* of love for fallen humanity, so that we "may all be one" (John 17:21). Perhaps Christ even sensed the open hands: "Father, into your hands I commend my spirit" (Luke 23:46).

Theologians call this self-gift of Christ on the cross *kenosis*, a Greek word that means self-emptying. It is the word used in Philippians 2:5–8:

> Let the same mind be in you that was in Christ Jesus, who, though he was in the form of God, did not regard equality with God as something to be exploited, but *emptied himself*, taking the form of a slave, being born in human likeness. And being found in human form, he humbled himself and became obedient to the point of death—even death on a cross. (emphasis added)

That is giving to an infinite degree. But did he receive? Was there a dynamic? Yes. Jesus trusted that he would receive the continued love and nourishment of the Father beyond his death, and he did. We cannot see the death of Jesus outside of the resurrection. But even beyond the resurrection, he went to his death knowing that choosing to give up his life would bring forth new life for humanity. He offered his life trusting that this horrible gift of dying was intensely fruitful.

And then, as he promised, he sent to humanity his Advocate, the Holy Spirit. The dynamic of giving and receiving is the only way we can understand the relationship of love the Son of God has with the Father, the Holy Spirit, and humanity.

The Holy Spirit: The Lord, the Giver of Life

In the Creed, we name the Holy Spirit as the Lord, the Giver of Life. Immediately you may see the relevance to the gift of birth! But for now, we focus on the Holy Spirit himself. The Holy Spirit is the "most high gift of God" (*donum Dei altissimum*) and the One who teaches us how to give and to receive.

St. Augustine, working from Scripture, argued that the Holy Spirit is God's gift of himself to humanity: "He is given as the gift of God, in such a way that he, as God, is himself the giver giving himself."[23] It sounds like a tongue twister, but we ought to see it as a mind twister: God gives himself to us in the Holy Spirit (remember, we are "temple[s] of the Holy Spirit"[24]), and that same Spirit teaches us to receive and give ourselves to God and to others. The Holy Spirit taught the frightened apostles to run into the streets of Jerusalem and proclaim the Good News. He taught the persecuted Christians what to say in court. He teaches us to trust God's plans through his peace and consolation. And, most of all, as Love Himself, he teaches us to love God and each other. Love always bears fruit.

Fr. Raniero Cantalamessa says that marriage, as the sacrament of reciprocal self-giving, is special witness to the life and work of the Holy Spirit.[25] As we continue, we will attempt to invite the Spirit with open hands into our reflections on the gift of childbirth.

For prayerful reflection

1. When you pray, take some time to pay attention to the position of your hands. Many people pray with hands gently clasped together as a sign of internal recollection. But when your hands are open in front of you, do you sense a different openness in communication? Try to pray with hands clenched. Is it even possible?

2. "In the end, a life of prayer is a life with open hands—a life where we are not ashamed of our weakness but realize that it is more perfect for us to be led by the Other than to try to hold everything in our own hands." (Nouwen, *With Open Hands*, 158). Ask the Lord what you are unconsciously clutching in your hands, what needs to be let go—especially in relationship to an impending birth.

3. What does it mean to be a temple of the Holy Spirit? In Jesus's time, the temple of Jerusalem was understood to be the

earthly home of the God of Israel. But when Jesus died on the cross, the curtain that separated that home (the Holy of Holies) from the rest of the Temple tore in half, "releasing" the Spirit of God. After Pentecost, the Spirit resides in the temple of each human being. Write out what it means for you to serve as a temple of the Holy Spirit: how you carry yourself, what you do, what you say.

4

"Lord, Teach Me to See": How Do We See the Holy Spirit in Giving Birth?

Birdwatchers are a marvel to me. I have no real experience birdwatching, but when I go birdwatching with someone who knows what they are doing, I stand back in amazement. We're walking around, and I see trees and sky and the occasional squirrel darting about. They see more. They know where to look, and voila: birds. Not just birds, but specific species, male and female, in molt or not. I hear a cacophony of bird calls; they hear individual songs and can say, "This one species is nearby." When the bird is sighted, there is a smile of wonder and pleasure. They see and can enjoy what I usually cannot.

And yet the birds are *right there*. I know it is a matter of practice, learning to see through the environment and find the bird. The Holy Spirit is "right there," too—but we don't always know how, or where, to look. We need to be taught, by the Holy Spirit himself, where to see God at work in our lives.

We begin by learning to pay spiritual attention.

God is actively preparing us for giving birth

Every child is desired and designed by God, a moment and reality in God's great plan of creation and salvation. If every child is desired by God, does it not make sense that every mother is being prepared by God to give birth and be a mother? We mothers and future mothers are his children as well. God doesn't just want the goodness of the new baby; he also wants goodness for the baby's mother. Gestation and giving birth have their challenges, but they are also windows to the work of the Giver of Life. Our role, as birthing mothers, is to cooperate with the Holy Spirit as we can to give birth to this child, created as a son or daughter of the King of Kings. It is an awesome responsibility, and comes with real joy—a gift of the Holy Spirit.

So how are we prepared, not just to receive a child, but to give birth? Much of this book encourages us to *pay attention* to specific moments that women have felt are encouragements, consolations, and challenges to bear. For example, the first time you hear your baby's heartbeat, you know: that moment is bigger than any medical notation of the heart rate. It is usually your first tangible evidence that there is a living child in your womb, with a beating heart, just like yours. Many parents react with a smile of wonder and pleasure.

Learning to "behold"

Pay attention to the "wow" moments. They are gifts, and meant to prepare you for birth. They become part of the tapestry that makes up the gestation and birth of this child, as well as your motherhood. They become part of your story, your life in the Holy Spirit.

The scriptural term for "to see with attention" is *behold*. And a common philosophical term for long, loving beholding is to *gaze*.[26] This is a time where we are called to gaze upon our lives. It is a time where, if we cannot see the work of the Holy Spirit in our calling to give birth, we can learn to ask the Spirit to help us see. Unlike the elusive bird the bird-watcher seeks, the Holy Spirit *wants* us to see, *wants* to be found. Sometimes, with a simple request, the branches of our lives simply brush away and we see the Spirit in his glory.

Birdwatchers look and listen for bird calls, fluttering, darts of color, and other patterns that point to the elusive bird. Those of us looking for the Holy Spirit begin by looking for senses of wonder, peace, joy. No evil spirit can mimic these, and human interest, contentment, and pleasure pale by comparison. Where wonder, peace, or joy is found—stay there. It is meant to be savored with gratitude. After all, it is a gift.

But also pay attention to sadness, anxiety, and confusion. Childbirth is not only challenging, it is fallen (see ch. 5). Most women do not walk around in perpetual bliss throughout their pregnancies. Beyond the everydayness of it (for nine months, anyway), impending birth and parenting can awaken every fear in the book. Fear of this type does not come from God. But now is an excellent time to practice the lifelong work of handing over your fears to God, rather than letting them define your life.

This kind of paying attention to the spiritual realities in our lives is sometimes called *living with a contemplative attitude.* Contemplative prayer is about receiving the Holy Spirit; instead of speaking to God (discursive prayer), contemplative prayer is about listening to God. A contemplative attitude is about fostering a life that listens or looks for God in the ordinary details of daily living. You keep living your life, but with one eye slightly squinted, always on the lookout for the Holy Spirit. The more you do it, the easier it becomes (the Holy Spirit is not hiding, right?). I encourage you to use this pregnancy, or your remembrance of a recent pregnancy and birth, as a place to foster a contemplative attitude. This attitude is where we learn to give and to receive, where we become students of the Holy Spirit. This giving, receiving, and cooperation with the Holy Spirit will also help us learn how to give birth.

For prayerful reflection

Has there been a time in your life where you have sensed the peace of God? Sensing a "peace beyond understanding" (Philippians 4:7) is one of the classic markers of discernment (the process of trying to make a decision that involves God's will). Often people sense a strong awareness of the peace of God after reconciling with God in the sacrament of Reconciliation.

If you can recall such a time, try to bring the details of the experience to mind: what led up to it, the experience of peace, words to describe it, any gratitude or lasting effects. Write these remembrances down, asking the Holy Spirit what you could learn from this memory, and how to recognize the Spirit's work again.

5

Wait—Isn't Birth Supposed to Hurt?

At this point, you may be thinking, "She's forgotten something. . . ."

All this lovely talk of new life, mutual self-gift, the dynamic of giving and receiving as a marker of the Christian life, the help of the Holy Spirit throughout . . . it all sounds graced and blissful. But wasn't one of the consequences of the sin of Adam and Eve that she would have pain in childbirth?

This claim is rooted in the text of Genesis 3, the story of the Fall of the first man and woman, and particularly in Genesis 3:16–19. Here is how the New Revised Standard Version translates the text:

> To the woman he said,
> "I will greatly increase your pangs in childbearing;
>   in pain you shall bring forth children,
> yet your desire shall be for your husband,
>   and he shall rule over you."
>
> And to the man he said,
> "Because you have listened to the voice of your wife,
>   and have eaten of the tree
> about which I commanded you,
>   'You shall not eat of it,'
> cursed is the ground because of you;
>   in toil you shall eat of it all the days of your life;
> thorns and thistles it shall bring forth for you;
>   and you shall eat the plants of the field.

By the sweat of your face
  you shall eat bread
until you return to the ground,
  for out of it you were taken;
you are dust,
  and to dust you shall return."

When the text is translated in this way, it is no wonder that readers are left with the impression that pain is a necessary consequence of the sin of the first humans. But there is good reason to believe that *pain* (or *pangs*) is not the best word to use.

Toil or pain?

The Theology of the Body says that men and women were created for mutual self-giving, a complete and total gift of self that was designed to be crowned with new life. But with the original sin, relationships became twisted, and fear, shame, and toil came into the world. We are still created to live according to the law of the gift. But the relationships designed in a perfect order prior to the Fall—God to humanity, man and woman to one another, and man to the earth—are broken as a consequence of that Fall, that concrete choice to want to be God rather than human. Now, man tills the earth with toil and struggle. Woman gives birth in *eseb* (commonly translated *pain*, but wait . . .), and yet her desire is for her husband, who lords over her. The man and woman realize they are naked and vulnerable and clothe themselves in order to protect themselves from one another's objectifying looks. And God recognizes they cannot be trusted, and for their own good, casts them from the garden that contains the tree of life. Eating a fruit that would immortalize grievously broken relationships would be no blessing.

But let's look more closely at the consequence borne by Eve and all women: that she would give birth in *eseb*. It is a tragic consequence, because it strikes at the very heart of a primordial relationship: it leads the mother to fear the birth of her own child. But what most people remember is this: childbirth gets identified with pain.

There is no question: sometimes, childbirth is painful, even extremely painful. But childbirth is not identified with physical pain in Genesis. Let's look at the original Hebrew:

What God says to Eve:

> To the woman he said, "I will greatly increase your pangs [*issabon*] in childbearing; in pain [*be'eseb*] you shall bring forth children. . . ." (Gen 3:16)

What God says to Adam:

> . . . [C]ursed is the ground because of you; in toil [*issabon*] you shall eat of it all the days of your life . . . . (Gen 3:17b)

Both Adam and Eve receive pronouncements that one result of sin is *eseb* (*issabon* comes from the Hebrew root *eseb*). *Eseb* is a word commonly used in the Hebrew Scriptures—yet every other time but one, it is translated as *toil.*[27] While toil certainly refers to exertion and hard work (and pain and exhaustion can be a part of that, as well as frustration and sorrow) the first meaning of *eseb* is not pain; it is work.

When birthing is associated with pain in the Greek language Scriptures, there is a similar disconnect. The Greek word *lupe* is used there, and translated into English as *pain.* But *lupe* refers to emotional challenge, not physical pain. The Septuagint, an ancient Greek translation of the Jewish Scriptures,[28] uses the Greek *lupe* to translate the Hebrew *eseb*—further evidence that *eseb* is not primarily about physical pain.[29] *Lupe* is also used to refer to birth in the New Testament, in John 16:21–22:

> When a woman is in labor, she has pain [*lupe*], because her hour has come. But when her child is born, she no longer remembers the anguish [*thlipsis*] because of the joy of

> having brought a human being into the world. So you have pain [*lupe*] now; but I will see you again, and your hearts will rejoice, and no one will take your joy from you.

Thlipsis is a word that means applying pressure, compressing (which is a remarkably accurate descriptor for labor contractions). Once again, pain *could* be a consequence of pressure. But it is not the root meaning of the word.[30]

Toil—hard, total exertion and work—is the meaning of birth after the Fall. And while toil can and often does entail physical pain, it does not *always* do so.

Can the sign be seen through toil? Or pain?

In short, yes, it can. The reason for addressing these Hebrew details is to help you understand that pain is not the primary definition of pregnancy—even a pregnancy after the Fall. Openness to life and the work of the Holy Spirit is. And it is possible to have that be the visible focus of your birthing.

It is important to realize that a childbirth that involves hard work, but not necessarily soul-crushing pain, is possible. Not guaranteed, but possible. Understanding that toil and anguish may be part of our inheritance of the Fall may help us prepare for birth differently. But second, it is important to recognize that God does not give people pain. If there is pain, it exists as part of the reality of our fallen existence and broken relationships, one of the consequences of original sin. God created us for love and for that love to bring forth new life. That should be our focus. There is no biblical mandate to embrace the pain.

In most cases, we should avoid the worst pain as we can, in order to facilitate a better mother-and-child beginning. But if that is not possible, at least recognizing that pain is not part of God's original plan, and asking for the strength to endure it—or offering it as a sharing in Christ's passion—is a meaningful step.

Finally, as I mentioned in the introduction, this book does

look at natural childbirth as the default way that women give birth worldwide. I should be clear: it is not wrong to make a decision with your doctor or midwife to take advantage of anesthetics, such as an epidural. Epidurals can help, medically and psychologically, in some cases. But there are medical disadvantages to such anesthesia as well. If you intend to try a natural childbirth, know that there are ways of reducing the pain of a typical childbirth that do not involve drugs—positioning, water immersion, back massage, relaxation techniques—and I personally would encourage mothers to take advantage of all these natural pain reduction options. Many women will vouch that they can work very well, changing birth from "extremely painful" to simply "hard work."

The piece to remember is this: even if your birth is painful, the Holy Spirit still abides with you and your child. God is present, and we are created for the Law of the Gift. God gives himself to you in the Holy Spirit, and you give yourself to your child through giving birth—even a fallen, toil-filled birth. Especially in a toil-filled birth.

For prayerful reflection

1. Make a list of all your fears about the physical and emotional aspects of childbirth. Then make a list of all you hope for in the physical and emotional aspects of your impending childbirth. Ask God to help you address the fears and not focus too much on your hopes, beyond living for God's will while giving birth.

2. The translations of *eseb*, *lupe*, and *thlipsis* to the single English word "pain" indicate a certain "reading into" the passages borne on the English-speaking world's preconceptions that childbirth must be painful. Read those passages cited with the words *toil*, *anguish*, and *pressure* for the three words above, respectively. Does this change your reading of the passage? If so, how?

6

Your Spiritual Keys in the Process of Giving Birth: Relax, Cooperate, and Yield to God

If "paying attention" is a large part of perceiving the sign of birth, and if gestation and giving birth were designed by God to help you spiritually grow closer to him, is it really as simple as opening our eyes and looking?

In a sense, yes. But perhaps you were in elementary school, sitting in a desk doodling in your notebook, and you didn't notice that the class had moved on to another topic. "Pay attention!" your teacher scolded. Well, your eyes were open and you *were* paying attention . . . to your doodle. The challenge is to *what*—or *Whom*— should we pay attention? There are three spiritual keys to living out a contemplative attitude that can help you "pay attention" in your pregnancy and beyond. Following are the three spiritual keys to giving birth:

1. Relax and give God permission to work in your life.

This little gem comes from Fr. Bob Sears, SJ, and when I first heard him say it, I thought it was simplistic. But it is actually genius. In opening the day by praying, "God, I give you permission to work in my life," you are deliberately announcing your openness to God. You are saying you are open to God's will. And you are saying you are ready to receive the Holy Spirit. Of course, God doesn't need your permission to work in your life. But he wants it, because he will not force his will on you; he respects your freedom.

The second piece is to relax. Our God is a giver of good gifts. He is also providential, and the Holy Spirit is Love Itself. You may know circumstances are hard. But to relax is to make an act of trust in God. There is no better place to be than in God's hands, no matter the challenges. You can, and should, relax.

2. Cooperate with God's intention to realize your motherhood through your body now.

If the first key boils down to "be ready to receive," the second key is to "be ready to give." One of the elements of motherhood is to welcome your child and make room for him or her in your life. Indeed, this begins during pregnancy with your very body: your body was designed to carry a child, but there is no question it gets uncomfortably crowded in the last trimester. You give room. You cooperate by doing what you can to nurture this unborn child. You eat relatively well, you stop smoking or drinking, you talk to the child and pray for the child. And you prepare for birth, spiritually and physically, as you can.

As we move forward in the following chapters, I will ask you to consider: At each point of giving birth, how is your birthing body given in love? That question may help you focus on the practice of self-gift.

3. Practice yielding to the Holy Spirit.

Yielding is a wonderful word in this context. It can refer to fruitfulness (such as a field yielding a crop), but for this third key, I use the more common understanding of the word: to bend or give way. As the Lord and Giver of Life, the Holy Spirit is much of the raw power behind the act of giving birth, and we mothers yield to that power through how we handle contractions and pushing. Contractions typically begin very gently, but by the end can have the intensity of a tidal wave. It is best to learn how to yield to and cooperate with that power rather than stand against it. To brace yourself against a contraction is like bracing yourself against a tsunami: it does not work. There are concrete ways we can try to yield to the work of God in this event. Before birth, praying for an increased ability to yield to the Holy Spirit is a beautiful act of Christian discipleship which will bear fruit beyond the birthing event.

So, am I praying my way through this childbirth?

Well, you certainly *could* pray your way through. Many women do, including women who do not consider themselves particularly religious. Many people name giving birth as one of the most spiritual events in their lives. Prayer is a natural way to respond to a spiritual event.

Having said that, if you see prayer in terms of some formal ritual that must be observed in a particular fashion, in a particular order, with a particular reverence, you may be setting false expectations as to what birth is like. Giving birth is often unpredictable—some women give birth quickly, some slowly. The birth may be medically uncomplicated, or serious medical challenges may arise. Some women experience little pain, and others a lot. Some births are quiet, with an attendant and a spouse, others have a medical cast of thousands. Personally, I would suggest having a birth plan (a list of preferred medical practices within the birthing process, filed with your medical provider before the birth). But I would avoid making a spiritual plan other than these spiritual keys. If suggestions are made in the following chapters that you want to adopt, please do so. But part of paying attention to the activity of the Holy Spirit in helping you give birth involves knowing what is appropriate to the time. Usually, that is cooperating with the act of giving birth, and that is both a physical and prayerful occupation, enough for any birthing mother.

For prayerful reflection

1. As you may have noticed, these spiritual keys are appropriate to giving birth but may be employed at any time. Could you pray, "God, I give you permission to work in my life"? It is a short sentence, so take time to re-collect yourself, look within, and say the sentence slowly five to ten times, letting it sink in. This may help you to be more open to God's work. Then, could you relax? How would you relax as an act of trust in God?

2. It may help to add to your nightly prayer repertoire an "act of trust." This one is offered by Bishop Michael Sis[31]:

> Lord Jesus, I trust in you.
> I place my life in your hands.
> I place our world in your hands.
> I cannot know the future.
> Help me to trust that, no matter what future difficulties
> this world may bring, you will always be there,
> to give me the graces I will need in that moment.
> Help me to remember
> that you are already there waiting for me, in the future
> that I have yet to experience.
> I thank you for your protection
> and your love.
>
> Amen.

Reading the Signs of Birth

7

Choosing Wonder: The Conception of a Child

The Language of the Body

***Conception:* When a sperm burrows into the egg, the egg instantly changes so no other sperm can "get in," and a new human being comes into existence, complete with a unique "blueprint" written into his or her DNA. At the moment of conception, this new person receives a soul from God, created for that person by God. He or she then travels out of the fallopian tube and implants in the woman's uterus. As the embryo continues to grow at an astounding pace, the mother's hCG hormone levels increase, and can be measured by a pregnancy test nine to ten days after conception.**

One of my "you're pregnant" moments has to be chalked up to God's rich sense of humor. I was on an eight-day silent retreat as part of my spiritual direction preparation program, and my question moving into the retreat was, "What does God want of the next phase in my life?" I was considering many things, but I fully did not expect to be pregnant. So when the signs kept adding up while I was on retreat, I finally picked up a pregnancy test from a store in town. I fully intended to take the test, learn I was not pregnant, and rededicate myself to this retreat. The next morning I took it and walked away, still thinking the odds were laughably slim. Then I picked up the test and saw the two parallel lines: pregnancy. I just stood there and gawked, literally speechless (but it was a silent retreat, so that worked!). An hour later, I met with my friendly Jesuit director for a previously scheduled meeting, where the exercises of the day were quickly scuttled for absorbing this news—and emotionally, I was all over the map. I do remember him saying quietly, after I had lapsed into more speechlessness, "You're carrying a child who may change the whole world"—a statement that reminded me that what was happening was much bigger than my own life. The next day I asked him if he had ever had anyone announce a pregnancy during a spiritual exercises retreat, and he smiled and said, "Since I usually work with priests and religious sisters, no, you're definitely the first!"

How did you receive the news "you're pregnant"?

Most women take a pregnancy test and see the "double line" sign pop up in the tiny results window. Some realize they missed a period and after a few days, come to the likely conclusion. Others who are expert at Natural Family Planning realize that their temperature has been slightly elevated for days now and is not dipping down, a sign of pregnancy.

But *emotionally*, how did you receive that amazing, life-altering news? Did you rejoice, like Hannah and Elizabeth? Were you delighted? Relieved? Grateful? Amazed? Or—honesty is key here—shocked? Upset? Frightened? In denial? Even angry? A combination of many of these reactions?

Note that none of those reactions are casual. This is a big event, and your body and soul know it. You are no longer one, but two. Another person has been created by God to live with him in his Kingdom. That's not in the future—that is now, and as close as your own heartbeat. Imagine: God's love has broken into the world and is living in the very center of yourself. You've only just discovered it, like the hidden treasure in the field.

These emotional reactions, whatever they may be, tell you

where you are at. Sometimes emotions are more accurate than the spoken word. Can you imagine saying you are upset about this pregnancy, and yet also being unable to repress a small spurt of joy at the thought? Or saying you are happy, and your stomach is a twisted knot of worry?

There may be valid sources behind every emotional reaction you are experiencing. But let's look at one way of receiving this news that might help you calibrate your own reaction: how Mary accepted the pregnancy of Jesus.

Fear or wonder: I get to choose?

> In the sixth month the angel Gabriel was sent by God to a town in Galilee called Nazareth, to a virgin engaged to a man whose name was Joseph, of the house of David. The virgin's name was Mary. And he came to her and said, "Greetings, favored one! The Lord is with you." But she was much perplexed by his words and pondered what sort of greeting this might be. The angel said to her, "Do not be afraid, Mary, for you have found favor with God. And now, you will conceive in your womb and bear a son, and you will name him Jesus. He will be great, and will be called the Son of the Most High, and the Lord God will give to him the throne of his ancestor David. He will reign over the house of Jacob forever, and of his kingdom there will be no end." Mary said to the angel, "How can this be, since I am a virgin?" The angel said to her, "The Holy Spirit will come upon you, and the power of the Most High will overshadow you; therefore the child to be born will be holy; he will be called Son of God. And now, your relative Elizabeth in her old age has also conceived a son; and this is the sixth month for her who was said to be barren. For nothing will be impossible with God." Then Mary said, "Here am I, the servant of the Lord; let it be with me according to your word." Then the angel departed from her. (Luke 1:26–38)

We do not know much about how Mary gave birth to the infant Son of God, as Scripture is silent on any details beyond a birth in Bethlehem, with no room in the inn. But we do know and cherish this passage, Mary's acceptance of her unexpected charge, her first and only pregnancy. The angel says she will conceive and bear a son, the Son of the Most High—a stunning message. And Mary simply responds with a clarifying question: How can this be, since I am a virgin?

There is legendary material in the early Church that Mary was consecrated to God in the Temple as a child, and that this marriage to (a likely elderly) Joseph was understood from the beginning as a caretaking relationship.[32] Women did not live alone in this culture; and this sort of arrangement was unusual but not unprecedented. The passage supports this sense of a lifelong consecration through virginity, because the angel says she *will* (in the future) bear a son, and she responds by saying she is a virgin—how could this be, even in the future, if she is (and through her consecration, will be in the future) a virgin? This is important, because it underlines this point: Mary saw her life as completely dedicated to God. This pregnancy had to "make sense" in light of her dedication to God.

The other remarkable piece that we get from this Scripture is not just that Mary responds, but she responds *without fear.* There is no fear in this passage: some confusion, some pondering, some clarification. But her response in the end is quick and simple: "[L]et it be with me according to your word." Fearlessness is not a word often ascribed to Mary, but it fits. Grown men in Scripture have responded with more fear to God's call than did this young woman. Perhaps Mary was able to respond fearlessly and in peace because she was the eminent example of love for God. And as the evangelist John later says, "[P]erfect love casts out fear" (1 John 4:18).

Emotionally, the beauty of Mary's response is that her spirit of fearlessness—or better, call it a spirit of trust—opened the door to *wonder*. And wonder is one of the best and most fruitful dispositions any of us can take to the new life growing within us. Choose wonder. Take some time to ponder prayerfully the reality of this new little person, growing at an astounding speed, moving, wiggling, developing. Wonder at the fact that there is a new soul under your heart. Wonder that you have been called to be a mother, and in fact, you are *now* a mother. You have received a call. Circumstances may be desired or terribly difficult, but can you say, "Let it be . . ."? Can you trust God to unfold a path for you to walk?

"Let it be with me according to your word": On chosenness

The other piece that can be easily lost in absorbing the news that you hold a new life within you is that another announcement came with "you're pregnant"—that is, you are a mother. Not you *will be* a mother, but you *are* a mother. Even if you miscarry in the next hour, you are always and forever a mother.

Motherhood is a vocation. We are used to understanding the priesthood or religious life as a vocation, a calling from God. But through baptism, all people are called to discipleship, as well as to a particular vocation in life. There is a reason the marriage vows ask, "Will you accept children lovingly from God . . . ?" You declared an openness to new life and the fruitfulness that can come from the love between you and your beloved. Every sexual act presumes that openness to the gift of life.

If that language seems a little too heady for you, try this instead: God wants you to be a mother. The meeting of that sperm and that egg was not random. At the very moment you realized you were pregnant, God was busy knitting together the child in your womb to be beautifully, fearfully, and wonderfully made.

All vocations come from the Holy Spirit. The Spirit of God chose the prophets of old, calling them by name, and every prophet responded, "Here am I, Lord." And when we recite the Nicene Creed every Sunday, we name the Holy Spirit "the Lord, the Giver of Life." In a similar way, the Holy Spirit has worked perceptibly in your life, calling you by name to motherhood, accepting your offer of openness to life, and creating a new being for God's kingdom. You are chosen to carry this child, and to be a mother.

Note how Mary responded: "Here am I, the servant of the Lord; let it be with me according to your word." She responded like a prophet (Here am I), like a disciple (the servant of the Lord), and with acceptance (let it be). She did not resist her chosenness; instead, she trusted God. Do not question your abilities or worthiness. There is time to address what needs healing in your life. But the first step is to trust God.

Mary's Magnificat (Luke 1:46–55)

As we know, Mary went quickly to visit her relative, the older and presumed barren Elizabeth. Elizabeth's child (John the Baptist) leaps in her womb at Mary's approach, and Elizabeth remarks, "You had faith!" Mary's response is to turn the attention to God in a song of wonder and praise:

> "My soul magnifies the Lord,
> and my spirit rejoices in God my Savior,
> for he has looked with favor on the lowliness of his servant.
> Surely, from now on all generations will call me blessed;
> for the Mighty One has done great things for me,
> and holy is his name.
> His mercy is for those who fear him
> from generation to generation.
> He has shown strength with his arm;
> he has scattered the proud in the thoughts of their hearts.
> He has brought down the powerful from their thrones,

and lifted up the lowly;
he has filled the hungry with good things,
and sent the rich away empty.
He has helped his servant Israel,
in remembrance of his mercy,
according to the promise he made to our ancestors,
to Abraham and to his descendants forever."
(Luke 1:46–55)

Part of living without fear means trusting God. *Mary's song is a hymn of trust and joy* in the power and goodness of God. After all, why do we praise God? Yes, it is God's due. But it is also because when we sing in praise we open ourselves to God's inflowing life and goodness. To praise is to embrace the Holy Spirit. The Spirit of God himself helps us to put aside our doubt and fear, and to trust in God's plan for our lives.

For prayerful reflection

1. Close your eyes and remember the presence of our loving and healing God, fully present in your past and in your present. Invite the Holy Spirit to enter into the memory of receiving the news of your pregnancy. Remember the circumstances, the details, as much as you can.

> How does our loving God respond to your emotions? Where is God in this story?
>
> Can you imagine the Holy Spirit saying your name, revealing to you your pregnancy? Can you say, "Let it be with me according to your word"?
>
> Can you see now, if you didn't see then, that this discovery is a discovery of chosenness?

2. Read deliberately, slowly, with prayerful pauses, the "Magnificat" song of praise. Which line speaks to you? Repeat it in your mind, letting God speak to you and your life as one

called to motherhood. Journal or share this line, and why it seems to be important in your life with God.

> If you recently discovered you were pregnant, could you pray this prayer throughout your pregnancy?
>
> If the circumstances of your pregnancy are difficult, could you ask the Holy Spirit to teach you to sing this prayer? Could you ask Mary for help in praying it?

(If it is easier for you to pray with music, there is a wonderful contemporary rendition of the Magnificat available by David Kauffman named "Behold," available on iTunes, Amazon, and YouTube.)

8

Waiting: "How Long, O Lord?"

The Language of the Body

***Pregnancy:* The child grows at an exponential rate during this period, faster than at any point of his or her life. The mother may feel some "morning sickness," especially in the first trimester. The second trimester often comes with a sense of the baby's movement, and renewed energy for the mother. The third trimester becomes more challenging as the weight and size of the child impacts the mother's posture, breathing, sleep, and energy levels.**

"This is a fundamental dimension of man's existence, which is always a co-existence." —John Paul II[33]

Many remark that God knew what he was doing in making pregnancy nine months long; by the ninth month you are often willing to go through anything to get this growing child out! But the gestation of this child is a time with its own rhythm and beauty, and you will never live out the reality of coexistence more radically. It is also a time with its own challenges (there are women who find pregnancy much more difficult than the actual birth). This chapter reflects briefly on the more notable points.

First encounters: the ultrasound and the "quickening"

Not every woman in the Western world receives an ultrasound between sixteen and twenty weeks, but it is common. The ultrasound is used by technicians to ascertain how the baby is developing, assess the baby's age (in case that is unclear), and be aware of any potential challenges to the pregnancy or the baby's development. You may even learn whether the baby is a boy or a girl. All this means what you see, and how it is interpreted, can be great news or very hard news. It is a reality our ancestors did not have to deal with in their pregnancies. Most people hold that, in general, the advantages outweigh the disadvantages.

If you receive hard news in your ultrasound, you may wish to move to chapter 17. But for most women and men, the ultrasound is a moment of wonder (sometimes even when it is accompanied by hard news). I know seeing my child for the first time during the ultrasound struck me as a holy event, a gift from God that I did not fully expect to affect my soul to the extent it did. I was frankly speechless, and struck to the core by his beauty. Another mother described the holy gratitude of seeing her unborn child alive and kicking after a recent miscarriage:

> My first pregnancy was a loss, and seeing the little fluttering heart during my second pregnancy was a total blessing. I cried and thanked God that the baby was alive, and I've had similar reactions to every ultrasound I've had in subsequent pregnancies.[34]

Another mother describes a third-trimester ultrasound and the courage that seeing her child gave her to face a difficult birth:

> Because my pregnancy had been declared high risk, and they planned when he would be born, the doctor performed an ultrasound to verify my son was in the right position. It felt unreal; I looked, and I can still see that moment when he opened his eyes. It blew me away. I'd been scared about weathering the final stretch of induction, epidural, and birth, but once I'd seen his eyes, I knew I'd do it. I knew I could do anything for him.[35]

The other tangible moment of "meeting your child" during gestation is called "the quickening," that is, when the mother first feels the baby's movement. Most women are not sure that the first senses of movement are, in fact, the baby. But eventually it becomes clear: that movement that initially feels like a butterfly in your womb is your child. In a few days, the movement is strong enough to be shared with your husband or a close friend: "Hurry, feel, right here!" Later, you can "play" with your child by moving your hand to one side of your womb, and waiting to feel him move to cuddle next to your hand. (It's true! Try it!)

These first meetings make tangible what is real: there is a tiny new person growing inside of you, and she is announcing her existence. It is a quiet but real announcement: "Here I am, Mom." How do you respond?

The tiredness and the last, never-ending month

A few women glide through their pregnancies with good energy, exercising, working, and caring for other children with good grace and humor. And then there are the rest of us.

Pregnancy always made me enormously tired. Part of it may have been that I was pregnant in my 30s and 40s. But it is normal for women to feel more tired than usual, especially as you move into the third trimester and last weeks of the pregnancy. Your energy reserves are now expended for two, and the baby is growing at an astronomical rate.

The other difficulty many women have is that the baby's activity and movement always increases when you slow down (for example, go to bed). The walking and activity of the day lulls the baby to rest, and when you are quiet, baby thinks it is a great time to get some exercise. This can make it hard to sleep.

This reality of tiredness is both a gift and a sacrifice. On the one hand, tiredness is a gift in that it forces you to slow down a bit. Exercise and activity are important, but so is rest, and this is a time when you grab rest wherever you can. We honor marathoners more than we do pregnant women, but they are doing similar work in terms of long-haul exertion. Letting yourself rest—or at least lowering a few expectations—is a way to honor your own human dignity as a mother.

The tiredness is also a sacrifice. Most women enjoy being involved in their families and work and community, but this sapping fatigue makes it difficult. You may not be able to do all the things you hope to accomplish before giving birth to this baby. Try letting that expectation go, and consider it a small sacrifice. Making room for this growing child in your womb is real work and has real consequences. It's fine that your energy goes to your child for a few weeks. It is a temporary sacrifice, and your energy will come back.

In the meantime, pray for your child. Place your hand on your hidden child and ask the Holy Spirit to fill his heart. Receive the Eucharist at Mass knowing that at some level, your unborn child receives Jesus as well. Pray for the pregnancy: I prayed with Psalm 16, "Keep me safe, O God."[36] Tell your child you love him. Sing to him. Your relationship has already begun, even though your child's life is hidden for nine months. But the hidden life is a real and sacred life. Never forget!

For prayerful reflection

Chances are very good that part of your pregnancy falls within the season of Advent, the season of waiting for the Christ child. This can be a rich time to ponder the fullness of waiting. Even if it is not Advent, consider some of the music, the practices, the sense of Advent. Consider how waiting for the birth of Jesus can help you wait for the birth of this child. You may wish to pray through the following guided meditation.

Place yourself in a quiet space, and get as comfortable as you can make yourself. You may wish for a lit candle, to remember you live in the light of Christ.

With one hand on your womb and the other on your heart, ask God to help you imagine. . . .

This baby is attached to you, through the placenta, and swimming around, having a grand time. He or she can hear the sound of your heartbeat, your voice—they are extremely comforting, his first home. He swims some more. . . .

Although he or she is immersed in amniotic fluid, the baby does practice breathing. This is a good warm up for the birth to come, although he doesn't know that. He may even hiccup. She works those legs, those arms. Movement is fun! Let's keep it up. . . . Actually, the baby is getting tired now. Perhaps it is time for rest. . . .

She rests in your womb, content. This is home. She senses protection. She is free to thrive, to grow. . . .

As you are moved, pray for this little playful child. He has a soul and can receive the graces that we receive. She is within both your body and the Body of Christ. . . .

As your prayer ends, close with the opening lines of Psalm 16 (or another favorite prayer):

Protect me, O God, for in you I take refuge.
I say to the Lord,
"You are my Lord; I have no good apart from you."

Amen.

9

Opening: First Contractions

The Language of the Body

***First Contractions:* When labor begins, the baby's head is likely beginning to press down on the cervix, and continues to do so, effacing (or "flattening") and dilating (or "opening") the cervix. The contractions are muscular movements of the uterus, pushing the baby out, and causing the effacement and dilation. The amniotic sac of fluid may be cushioning the dilation. If a woman's water breaks early, that same effacement and dilation will occur without that cushion, probably more quickly but with greater intensity. The first emotional sign of labor, according to the Bradley Method, is excitement and happiness.**

My water broke in the middle of the night. I knew things likely wouldn't start right away, given my experience with water breaking and birthing Ben, and it would be best to rest as long as I could before labor began. I wanted Jerry to rest as well, so I didn't tell him, and I lay on my side as very mild contractions began to come, a few minutes apart. I was a little frustrated that my water broke, because I knew that likely meant a more difficult labor, but I was mostly happy and at peace that Julia was, ten days past the due date, finally on her way.

Once labor began, I spent a couple of hours trying to relax and ride the waves of contractions as they came, catnapping in between. The window began to lighten, the sun rose, and

I smiled, thinking, "And today is the day that Julia will be born."

THIS *is the day the Lord has made*

If the beginning of your labor is quiet and gentle, as mine was, it is wonderful to be able to take a moment and give thanks that today is the day your son or daughter will be born. Whatever the circumstances of your birthing, this moment of gratitude is necessary. There is a reason we honor birthdays; this is a big event.

Unless you and your doctor have chosen medical interventions, it is also a day whose arrival you cannot predict. You may have been given a due date or a "due zone" when the child is expected to be "at term," around thirty-seven weeks. If you go into labor before term, your medical provider may try to halt it. But if nothing is wrong, and birth is the simple result of gestation coming to an end, you can and should say:

> This is the Lord's doing;
> it is marvelous in our eyes.
> This is the day that the Lord has made;
> let us rejoice and be glad in it. (Psalm 118:23–24)

The psalmist was not talking about giving birth, but giving birth is the Lord's doing, and indeed this is the (birth) day that the Lord has made! Medical professionals admit that we do not know what triggers labor. There are signs when a woman is ready to begin labor, but no way to predict exactly when it will start. Indeed, we cannot even tell whether it is the baby who initiates labor or the mother, or some subtle interaction between them. The day you give birth is mysterious and the onset of contractions is the first visible move of the Holy Spirit. That is great reason to rejoice! In fact, the Bradley Method says that the first emotional sign in active labor is excitement and happiness.

What does it mean to give your body in love?

The Theology of the Body shows us how we are created for giving and receiving: the body is endowed with a spousal meaning that makes the body a sign that points to God. Active labor was given to us as a school in which we learn how to give and receive. Even through its fallenness, we can see active labor as meaningful. It is a natural consequence of the spousal meaning of the body, engaged and lived. The fruitfulness of the body is a sign that points to the Lord, the Giver of life, as well.

Remember, birth isn't always easy or joyful. But it is always meaningful, because God is there.

One way to live according to the Law of the Gift is to consider the question, "What does it mean to give your body in love?"[37] I'll raise this question throughout these chapters on active labor and pushing.

In the very beginning of labor, when typically the mother senses contractions 5–10 minutes apart, 30–60 seconds in length, much of your life can go on as normal. You can read, do some light cleaning, pack for the hospital, spend time with your other children, and so forth. (One time I baked a birthday cake for the baby, which my husband thought was slightly nuts, but he knew better than to stop me. Just don't leave the house suddenly without taking it out and turning off the oven. . . .) Reserve your energy a bit, and eat and drink lightly. If it is nighttime, try to sleep. The intensity of the contractions will wake you up when you need to get up.

It's all about opening

But "to give your body in love" at the beginning of labor means this is where you begin to open. Think about what your body is doing: you are giving way for the child to be born. The contractions at this point are not about pushing. The contractions are about opening. The muscles of your uterus "contract" as your child begins to bear down, opening your cervix millimeter by millimeter, like a head stretching out a turtleneck sweater. The contractions feel like waves, rising to a peak and then falling. (The word *birth* comes from an ancient word meaning "wave."[38]) A woman's womb, or uterus, is made up entirely of muscle, and that set of muscles flexes, flexes, flexes, and then relaxes. The goal here is to get to ten centimeters cervical dilation, at which point your body will move into pushing mode.

There are two things you need to do when having a contraction. One is to not be afraid—more on that in the next chapter. The other, which you can employ immediately, is to relax.

Relaxing is important because it allows your body to use all its energy and attention on the work of opening up. The Bradley Method is especially helpful on this point, and encourages mothers to very deliberately practice relaxing before birth. For example, clench a fist. Then release it. Note the difference in how you feel. When you go into a contraction, find positions to maintain that allow you to release tension everywhere in your body so you can concentrate on that one set of muscles opening up you focus on relaxing; and let the opening happen. Have a spouse or birth partner notice when tension is creeping up in other parts of your body (if your face is getting strained, a gentle touch or cool washcloth can release tension, or if your shoulders are getting tight, a light massage). You should try to be slack, even to the point of mimicking sleep, as much as reasonably possible during a contraction. That kind of relaxation, ironically, takes practice; it is good to rehearse relaxing your body frequently before a birth. In any case, most women have many contractions, so you'll get lots of practice!

But the spiritual element in this is key. You are relaxing

your body to make room for the work of birth. You are also relaxing your body as a sign of openness to the work of the Holy Spirit in bringing this child to birth. Ask the Holy Spirit to help you through the contractions, to help you open, to help the baby be born.

This makes it sound easy. For a few women, it is; but allowing the contractions to open your body to birth is an ongoing challenge for most women. If you begin to have difficulty, if the pain gets on top of you and prevents your relaxation, be calm, seek peace, and try again. We will focus more on challenges in the next two chapters. But early on, if you are lucky enough to begin labor gently, give thanks to our God, cherish these early contractions, and practice relaxing into the Spirit's work.

And employ your spiritual key: "Holy Spirit, I give you permission to work in my life." Then, relax.

For prayerful reflection:

1. There are many relaxation exercises found in Bradley Method books as well as in meditation books. If you hope to go into labor as relaxed as you can be, you would do well to practice these. Consider how you can "give God permission" to help you relax. Here's an adapted version of a practice relaxation exercise:

> St. Catherine of Siena was a deeply religious woman who decided not to live in a convent, but "in the world." She often spoke of communing with God not in a monastic cell, but in the "cell of her heart." Consider this a retreat into the cell of your heart.
>
> Lie down on your bed or get otherwise comfortable. Open your hands and the cell of your heart and say, "Here I am, Lord. I place myself in the light of Christ. I give you permission to work in my life. I ask: help me relax, help me trust in your love."

Focus on your toes on one foot and mentally clench them. Then release. Note what release feels like. Thank God for being able to relax your toes.

Focus on your toes on the other foot and tighten them in the same way. Release. Release a little more. Note the feeling. Again, thank the Holy Spirit for helping you relax.

Do the same with other muscles:

Calves

Full leg, one at a time

Hands

Biceps

Full arms

Upper back/shoulders

Lower back

Face: forehead, mouth, jaw

Finally, try to relax your entire body as much as possible.

End by praying these or similar words:

Thank you, Spirit of God, for preparing me for birth. Thank you for helping me be more open to your work in my life. Teach me to yield to your prompting and listen to your call. I ask this through Jesus Christ, our Lord.

2. Here is another visualization prayer to practice:

Visualize the Holy Spirit as he is symbolized in the Bible: as wind, or breath. Lie down, and deliberately place yourself in the light of Christ. Consider how Genesis 1:2, beginning an ode of creation, presents the Spirit of God: "Darkness covered the face of the deep, while a wind from God swept over the face of the waters."

How does the wind from God—perhaps a slight

movement of the breeze—on your skin, right now, relax you?

Can you sense the Holy Spirit through the moving, wrapping element of air, supporting you, supporting your child?

Can you sense the presence of the Holy Spirit in your own breathing, sustaining you and giving you life?

Lift your face to the wind, to the Spirit of God, and pray:

Come, Holy Spirit, fill the hearts of your faithful. Come, Creator Spirit. Help me follow your leading, and better yield to the One who is the Lord and Giver of Life. Help me relax and cooperate with your life-giving work.

10

Focusing on Love: Active Labor

The Language of the Body

***Active Labor:* Active labor occurs when the contractions are approximately one minute long and four minutes apart. At this point the contractions are stronger, more intensely felt, and more effective in bringing down the baby. The emotional sign for active labor is that the mother becomes very quiet and inwardly focused.**

[When I moved into active labor,] I really went inward and became very quiet when I felt a contraction coming and then that quiet became a small crescendo of groans. Ha! There were a few times I had to be reminded to take a breath and keep breathing. As far as spiritually, I may or (ahem) may not have said when I finally go home to gaze upon the beauty of Jesus, I will ask to meet Eve . . . so I can punch her in the face.
—Leann Putz

I was . . . at the alternative birth center, and it was quiet and peaceful . . . but it was a very positive experience. The breathing and being at liberty to move around freely made a HUGE difference . . . and during the worst of it, my midwife climbed up on the bed beside me and held onto me and breathed with me, and promised me I could get through it all. . . .

And I did.

Actually, the only "pain" I experienced was from the interferences, like being made to move, or internal checks during contractions. The rest of the time, it was strong and intense and powerful, but it didn't actually hurt.

I'll tell you what, though: They don't call it LABOR for nothin'.
—Laura L.

As I mentioned in chapter 5, the word Genesis 3 uses to describe women's contractions is often translated as *pain*, but it would be better translated *toil*. Pain *may* be a part of toil, but mostly, toil is hard, difficult work. And as women keep realizing, they don't call it "labor" for nothing.

Unless you have a Cesarean section, you probably cannot avoid the toil (although recovery from a C-section is a lot of work; it's major surgery). Labor, or work, is part of life. It is worth considering how to avoid undue pain, however.

Why is pain worth avoiding? Because it hurts? Yes, although we put up with other things that hurt. Because pain doesn't honor human dignity? Yes, but if we choose to undergo pain for another's sake, a person's dignity is not lost, but underscored. In giving birth, pain is worth trying to avoid with reasonable measures because it can shroud the sign of what is happening: the beauty of the woman giving of herself to give birth, with the help of others and the Holy Spirit, to new life. But if pain cannot be avoided, perhaps it can be accepted and offered for others.

In fact, look at Genesis 3 again, where God announces the consequences of Adam and Eve's original sin. Adam will till the land with toil and sweat to survive because his original relationship with the earth and its creatures has been fractured. Eve will give birth with toil, yet her urge will be for her husband, because her original relationship with her child and her husband has been fractured. Even the serpent loses his place of honor (as the most clever) and is placed in enmity with humanity. The result of original sin is broken relationships everywhere.

In contrast, giving birth can be a real sign of a right and healthy relationship, and was designed to be so. A man and a woman give themselves to one another in trust and love, and out of that love comes fruitfulness, manifest in this new person, this tiny body and great soul, given by God and received by the couple to love.

The problem with pain is that it can keep birthing mothers from seeing that this moment is part of the design of God and the work of the Holy Spirit. Pain is remarkably attention grabbing, and is an inheritance of original sin (the worst of "toil"). And our experience of giving birth is part of the fallen world. So when we are in labor, we are participating in the Law of the Gift, the dynamic of giving and receiving, a chance to live out our openness to God's work in our lives. But we also deal with the inheritance of toil.

The key here is to prepare for a birth that allows you to see the meaning of the moment. Take other things into consideration as well, of course, especially the health of yourself and the baby. But these two goods are not mutually incompatible.

In short, pain may happen, and learning how to alleviate it as much as possible is wise. Considering how to cope with it, medically, physically, emotionally, and spiritually, is also wise. But my main hope for you is this: Don't let pain distract you from being fully present at your childbirth. *Pain is not the last word of this event. Love and fruitfulness is.* Focus on that.

But how do you focus on love and fruitfulness?

Countering resistance and fear

You focus on love and fruitfulness by remembering the three spiritual keys:

- Give God permission to work in your life, and relax.
- Cooperate with God's intention to realize your motherhood through your body now.
- Practice yielding to the Holy Spirit.

Here is where the abstract becomes specific. In full-blown active labor, especially when you are contracting regularly and at six to nine centimeters dilation, the key is to relax your way through the contractions. Those contractions are going to happen whether you like it or not. Think about how to "stay out of the way" of your womb's work and allow the opening of your cervix to happen fully and efficiently. The increasing intensity of contractions can easily lead to fear of pain. But fear of pain keeps you from being fully present. How do you counter that? Try to relax. You can't relax and be afraid. Pray for that—but also let your relaxed body lead the way.

There are different ways to do this. Personally, I am partial to the Bradley Method of natural childbirth. Women who do Bradley, helped by their husband-coaches and perhaps a doula, spend significant time before birth learning to relax their muscles: if you can do that during contractions, it will hurt much, much less. Being in a position that allows gravity to help the child descend (upright, squatting, or sitting on a balance ball) can also help enormously, as long as you stay as relaxed as you can. You husband/coach's role is to keep you relaxed and encourage you. That may mean back massage, or wiping your brow, or calling awareness to the tension in your body and helping you release it. A fuller explanation can be found in books on the Bradley Method, or courses offered in your area.

Many midwives and some doctors also tout the pain-relieving advantages of water labor. Everyone alive knows the relaxing properties of taking a bath or floating in the water. Although not all hospitals or birth centers offer water birth (and it usually isn't offered to women who are high risk, simply because doctors want them closer to medical equipment), the benefits of water labor for pain reduction are huge. Submerging in the water, being able to float a bit, is key, so your home bathtub probably won't do it. You may wish to talk to your midwife or doctor about the pros and cons of doing water labor (or water birth).

Finally, there are different types of anesthesia, the most common being epidural anesthesia. Some women who really want a natural childbirth may not even want to consider it. But it is good to be prepared for anything. For example, if your child is in a very difficult physical position, and natural labor is exhausting you or putting you in such unnatural pain that you cannot effectively contract or push, an epidural may be the best option to facilitate a vaginal birth. Epidural anesthesia works well for pain relief and relaxing the lower body, but it comes at some cost as well. Again, talk to your medical professional about this option before giving birth.

Ultimately, cooperating with God's intention to realize your motherhood through your body involves discernment. God only wants you to do the best you can. Just remember that the Holy Spirit is fully present in that birthing spot, and turn to him for help. The best way to turn to the Holy Spirit is to practice *yielding* to the work of the Holy Spirit, and that is the theme of the next chapter.

For prayerful reflection

1. "Your weakness provides a place for God to break in, for God's mercy and God's power to animate your life. Can you be thankful for your weakness?" This gem came from a priest friend of mine, and seems especially relevant here. Giving and receiving birth is precisely about allowing God's mercy and power to animate your life and push your new child to birth. At some point during labor you will likely find this difficult. How can you pray, before you give birth, to thank God for any weakness that highlights how God's power can work in your life? List your weaknesses and ask God's mercy and power to address them, to let those weaknesses be places where God himself is revealed.

2. If you have already given birth, think about when you felt weak or overwhelmed. Where was God in that moment? If you do not know, prayerfully ask God to reveal how he was present in that moment.

11

Yielding to the Work of the Holy Spirit

Hard to think about, easier to do.[39]

Yield is more than a triangular sign on a freeway entrance ramp. It is actually a very rich word, especially when we are speaking about giving birth. To yield means to produce. For example, the land yields a crop. The tree yields good fruit. The earth yields abundance. One meaning of the word is actually "to bear fruit" . . . just as pregnant women do when they give birth.

Another meaning of the word is "to give place to another." Interesting that giving place to another is joined with fruitfulness, isn't it? But that is at the heart of what happens in active labor. Your body is opening, opening, opening: but you are not directly opening yourself. You are allowing the Holy Spirit and the baby, working together, to open your body in preparation for pushing the baby out into the waiting world, and into your arms. You are very much *giving place* to the baby and to the Lord of Life. Participating in the ongoing work of creation requires yielding to the Holy Spirit.

Yielding requires flexibility, a willingness to move, to adjust paths. Pregnancy, birth, and motherhood itself is like that: so this is a spiritual practice for the long haul. Let's consider what it means to practice yielding to the work of the Holy Spirit in active labor.

To yield is to adjust

There are certain ethical principles that must be observed in a birth: respecting the dignity of the child and the mother, taking due care to preserve the child's and the mother's health, remembering in some way that God is present. But beyond that, births look different, and you cannot completely predict how each one will go. Be flexible. You had your heart set on water labor, and the tub is already being used by someone else. Or an epidural, but it turns out you are too far into the labor to take advantage of it. Labor is a lot about living in the now and letting go of preferences and expectations. Your attention needs to be on God working through these contractions, riding those waves of power bringing you to birth. That's it. Yield to the will of God in the moment. Jean Pierre de Caussade's thoughts may help (see "For prayerful reflection," below).

To yield is to sound contractions

If you haven't given birth before, let me be candid: While it may or may not be painful, there is no escaping that it will be intense, especially later in the labor. Women who choose to do a natural childbirth without drugs may "make room" for the baby in part through groaning (or "sounding") through the most intense labor contractions. The Bradley Method suggests that releasing some of the intensity of labor through sound may be helpful to maintaining a relaxed state. Screaming, on the other hand, indicates you have lost that relaxed state. When the contraction is done, take a breath, try to relax again, and think low tones.

How is this yielding to the work of the Holy Spirit? If sounding helps you stay relaxed and allows the Giver of Life to work with you to open more so that the baby can descend closer to birth, then you are giving place. You are yielding to the work of God.

Not everyone is comfortable with sounding. That's okay. It isn't a necessity to giving birth. But it is so common that even St. Paul refers to the phenomenon: ". . . the whole creation has been groaning in labor pains until now . . ." (Romans 8:22). In fact, the way Paul cites the phenomenon, it is a kind of prayer. Could you think of that low intonation during challenging contractions as a kind of prayer—a participation in God's work and part of making room for God's power and love?

To yield is to trust in God

To say we trust in God is important. But how do we actively do that in the midst of timing contractions?

First, we can trust that God is present. It might help to keep something with you to remind you of God's presence: a picture, a candle, a prayer book, a rosary, a crucifix, or religious music are all possibilities.

Second, we can go into birth affirming that opening line of the Creed: "I believe in the Holy Spirit, the Lord, the Giver of Life." Our God is the Lord of birth. That is a remarkable statement! It's not us; it's not the doctors or nurses. The Holy Spirit is the Paraclete, or "he who is called to one's side."[40] What a wonderful title to remember when in active labor: the Holy Spirit is at your side, consoling you, helping you to give birth.

But sometimes the help of the Holy Spirit is supplemented by the help of others. Trust is a willingness to accept that help.

To yield is to accept help

Many women find doulas a great help in giving birth: indeed, many studies find that women who give birth with a doula alongside a medical professional have shorter and less medically augmented births.[41] It may be good to accept the reality that childbirth is challenging—and accept knowledgeable help in the form of a person advocating for you, making you comfortable, speaking for you to medical professionals. Human beings are the only mammals who do not as a matter of course give birth alone. We birth with others, for support and help. Employing a prayerful doula who can encourage your religious beliefs is even better.

The father of your child should also be there helping you give birth, if at all possible. While there is no question the woman does the lion's share of the work, women benefit from the support of their husbands. Do not take this time to blame your husband for your labor ("This is all your fault!" isn't very funny even on sitcoms). You two took vows, for better or for worse. Giving birth can be a mixture of both. This is something you do together. Allow him to help. If your baby's father cannot be there (if he is ill, or deployed, or you are a single parent) I strongly encourage you to invite a doula or a trusted friend or family member to be present at the birth. It is crucial to take seriously your need for support.

And yielding may also mean accepting the help of medical staff. You may not want to hear what the doctors or midwives have to say, especially if their suggestions go against your birth plan, but I would encourage you to give them a fair hearing. Almost always they simply want a healthy mom and a healthy baby. The other advantage of an experienced doula, however, is to double-check the medical advice you are getting. Medical staff are required to ask permission before a procedure, unless someone's life is in immediate danger. If medical staff recommend a procedure that you are uncertain about, remember that you can ask for a few minutes to consult with your husband, doula, and God.

For prayerful reflection

Yielding is often understood as a kind of surrender. One helpful description comes from the seventeenth century priest and spiritual master, Fr. Jean Pierre de Caussade:

> In this state of joyful self-surrender the only rule is the present moment. In this our soul is as light as a feather, liquid as water, simple as a child, as easily moved as a ball in following these nudges of grace. Such souls have no more consistence and rigidity than molten metal . . . so these souls are pliant and easily shaped to any form that God chooses to give them.[42]

Can you imagine yourself like a feather or a liquid—adjusting, moving, yielding to the nudges of the Holy Spirit? This can be a very useful way to imagine oneself while in labor. Let go and let God do the moving of the baby in you. Be as relaxed as you can be: you are in God's hands and the hands of others who care for you. Offer this labor, indeed all your labors, to the Holy Spirit. Letting God lead means being willing to live in the moment and practice yielding.

12

Trusting: The Transition from Contractions to Pushing

The Language of the Body

***Transition:* Transition occurs when the cervix is dilated 8-10 cm and fully effaced, moving labor from the end of the first stage (contractions) to the beginning of the second stage (pushing). The baby's head is at or near +0 station, which means he or she is "engaged," pressing down for the pushing stage. If the mother's water (amniotic fluid) has not broken yet, it usually will at this stage. The emotional signs of transition include seriousness and self-doubt. Contractions come quickly, lasting about a minute, sometimes with very little break in between. Many women find this stage painful, but it is also short, thirty minutes or less.**

You have worked with active labor for a while now, trying to relax, trust, and ride the contractions like waves. You're far along at this point, and the contractions are at their most intense. Suddenly, you're confused, unsure, staring blankly at people. You are expressing the expected "sign of self-doubt."

The sign of self-doubt may be the first thing you have read so far that gives you pause. People who give birth according to the Bradley Method actually learn to recognize this sign and turn it into a positive: the coach, doula, or savvy medical professional will often counter, "You are doing so well, and you are getting *really* close to holding your baby. This is nearly the end, you're handling this wonderfully! You can do this!"

But the mother's statement that elicits such an affirmative reaction is a tough one: "*I don't think I can do this.*"

Why the self-doubt, suddenly? Even the woman who is a rock star at handling labor is prone to make such a statement, or at least think it, in this phase of transition. Thank goodness it is a very short phase (perhaps thirty minutes at most). But still.

There is no question this phase is intense. The contractions are hard, it is increasingly hard to relax, and the probability of painful work is high. The "rest time" between contractions is briefer. All the relaxation techniques and posture cues still help, but it may feel less like it. Basically, your uterus is now working at full capacity and speed to get the cervix dilated and the baby ready for birth. It is good, and not a sign of something wrong, but it is hard. One way to think of it: literally, there is no way out but through. You need to commit to it. And that means trying to relax every muscle, letting the uterus do its work, and in that relaxation, opening yourself to the help of God.

If you have an epidural, most of the physical challenge of this stage may be missed. But you can still give yourself in love in a deliberate way by relaxing, praying, and visualizing your cervix opening and the Holy Spirit working to bring forth new life.

What does it mean to give oneself in love?

That signal of "self-doubt," I would argue, is a spiritual observation. It is a recognition of what St. Francis de Sales calls "self-abjection."

Self-abjection? *That* is a loaded word. But it is basic to the Christian life. To consider oneself abject is to recognize oneself as poor, without the resources to save one's own life. And at this point in labor, it fits: the mother is usually very tired and without reserves, and recognizes that what is asked of her—to work through the most difficult part of the labor—feels, and may well be, completely beyond her. It is a recognition of her poverty, that she needs help. It is a loaded word, but it is an accurate assessment of her spiritual reality. In fact, it is a window into every human being's spiritual reality: we need God.

If you have a coach or doula, you could ask them to affirm you in this manner, if you express self-doubt rooted in that poverty: "You can do this with the help of God. God is going to see you through this. You are safe, and the medical team is making sure you and the baby are safe. You can do this with God's help." Coaches or doulas could pray with you. I strongly recommend keeping it simple and short, because as soon as a contraction begins again, you are going to need to focus on relaxing and sounding the contraction.

Another prayerful way to handle transition, whether you are birthing naturally or with the help of an epidural: give your birthing work, everything in the moment, to God. Your husband or doula could remind you: "The Holy Spirit is helping you and is *right here*. Give it to God. You are opening up, your body is doing hard work. You are almost there. Put any self-doubt in a box and give it to God." If you typically pray to Jesus Christ, or God the Father, or a saint, it may be appropriate to address your prayer during transition in the same way. But to pray to the Holy Spirit as "the Lord and Giver of Life" may be especially meaningful here.

If you have been working with water imagery, "riding the waves" of contractions—or if you are doing a water birth—remembering that the Spirit surrounds you like water, and that you yield to the Spirit of God surrounding you and your child in this birth, may also be powerful.

Does the Holy Spirit pray through you?

The previous chapter mentioned that "sounding" (or groaning) may be helpful in yielding to the contractions, especially if the mother is able to vocalize the contractions with a low moan—the open mouth and low tone helps the mother stay relaxed and release stress. But could it also be a prayer of poverty? We don't need to pray through words; in fact, St. Paul said himself that the Spirit intercedes for us when we do not know how to pray:

> We know that the whole creation has been groaning in labor pains until now; and not only the creation, but we ourselves, who have the first fruits of the Spirit, groan inwardly while we wait for adoption, the redemption of our bodies. . . . Likewise the Spirit helps us in our weakness; for we do not know how to pray as we ought, but that very Spirit intercedes with sighs too deep for words. And God, who searches the heart, knows what is the mind of the Spirit, because the Spirit intercedes for the saints according to the will of God. (Romans 8:22–23, 26–28)

If you have given birth previously: Could you prayerfully imagine the Holy Spirit, the One who initiates all prayer,[43] as the One helping bring you to birth—in part, through your sounding? If you anticipate giving birth, are you willing to stand with St. Paul and recognize these "groanings" or "sighs" as your prayer? It may be a lament, it may be yearning, it may be self-abjection vocalized. But it is the Holy Spirit's gift and his work through you to pray in this way.

It may be a radical change to not just pray to God, but to open yourself to *allow the Holy Spirit to pray through you.* Self-abjection calls us to lean on God, to relax into God. Your body has been fearfully and wonderfully made, but He alone is trustworthy.

For prayerful reflection

1. The key to handling transition in an unmedicated birth is to know what to expect: a short but very intense and possibly

painful phase of contractions where you may begin to doubt you can do this. Medical staff and doulas can address pain with positioning, water submersion, and some anesthesia options. But going into transition with a "spiritual bag of tricks" is wise. How will you pray? Will you ask others (in the birthing room or away) to pray?

2. Can you practice a prayer during your relaxation exercises that imagines the Holy Spirit working with and through you? All while supporting you? It stretches the imagination, but God will do that, whether you are in pain or not. Our problem is not that we make God too big, but that we make God too small. As St. Teresa of Avila said, ask God great things; it flatters him!

3. You may want to add this prayer to your "spiritual bag of tricks" as a way of reminding you of God's strength when you are weak. This snippet comes from a hymn commonly called "The Breastplate of St. Patrick"[44]:

> I arise today, through God's strength to pilot me:
> God's might to uphold me, God's wisdom to guide me,
> God's eye to look before me, God's ear to hear me,
> God's word to speak for me, God's hand to guard me,
> God's way to lie before me, God's shield to protect me,
> God's host to secure me:
> against snares of devils, against temptations of vices,
> against inclinations of nature, against everyone who
> shall wish me ill, afar and anear, alone and in a crowd.
>
> . . .
>
> Christ with me, Christ before me, Christ behind me, Christ in me,
> Christ beneath me, Christ above me,
> Christ on my right, Christ on my left,
> Christ in breadth, Christ in length, Christ in height,

Christ in the heart of every man who thinks of me,
Christ in the mouth of every man who speaks of me,
Christ in every eye that sees me,
Christ in every ear that hears me.

13

Cooperating with God: Pushing and Letting Birth Happen

The Language of the Body

***Pushing*: The mother is now using her muscles in a different way in this second stage. No more opening up—now she can concentrate on pushing the baby out. Otherwise there are similarities: contractions may last one minute, and then the mother is given approximately a three-minute break. This stage is almost always shorter than the first stage, and sometimes exceedingly short (mere minutes). The emotional signs mirror those in first stage labor: excitement, then seriousness, then self-doubt.**

> With my [sixth child], she popped out while I thought I needed to go to the bathroom before the midwife checked my dilation. . . . I truly did not even really "feel" [the baby] being born . . . she just came out and I was in a state of euphoria. I grabbed her head to cushion [it] and my midwife then ran into the bathroom and grabbed the rest of her and I shouted, "Is that it? That was awesome!"
> —Carla

> It took a while to learn how to push but when it hit, it hit! The bewildering combination of being compelled to push juxtaposed against the very real sense that doing so will split one in two is the hardest to overcome. Because of this I felt like I was pushing toward my own death, like I might die if I continue but I couldn't NOT continue. Looking back on it, I suppose in a certain sense I was dying, if only in the

> sense where I died to that part of myself which would keep me from caring for this child.
> —Jennifer Wendt

The experience of pushing can be the most variable part of giving birth. Mothers who have not given birth often think pushing is the hardest part. In my experience,[45] it was not. I thought it much easier than what I had just experienced, a common feeling for women going through natural childbirth.

But other women experience the pushing stage as very challenging: it is often fast, and sometimes the speed of the baby descending can be painful, hard work. Huge babies, and babies out of position, can create demanding pushing experiences. But regardless, pushing is a cause for celebration and relief. You are getting so very close!

Many women, especially those doing natural childbirth, experience a few minutes of calm in "the eye of the storm" between contracting and pushing. If you get this quiet time, relax (it will be easier to relax now) and rest a bit. This is a gift. Rest and get into the position you want to be in for pushing.

This second stage of pushing mirrors the first stage in terms of emotional signs: the birthing mother is excited, then internally focused and working hard, then finally pushing through some self-doubt. It's just a shorter stage. Let me walk through a typical pushing stage with you.

Chosenness

Instead of relaxing and allowing your body to open, in the pushing stage your focus turns toward actively cooperating as the muscles of your uterus work like a piston to push the baby down and out. If you are like most women, it may take some practice to get the hang of cooperating with your body in this work. You may decide to change positions, breathe differently, and so forth.

The pushing stage, like conception, is a moment of chosenness. Despite jokes about the "impossibility" of pushing a baby out, in fact a woman's body is created to do this very thing. We are not being asked to do the impossible; indeed, *we were designed for this*. Every time a nurse says, "You can do this," it isn't a false encouragement—it's true! It may be hard, but it is true. God calls you to this moment and is pushing right behind that baby. You are chosen to do this.

Cooperating

Feeling the baby move down your birth canal is a strange sensation and definitely hard work. But other than that, the "waves" are similar to the first stage of contracting: push, more, more, MORE, less, less, now rest a minute. Wait for the signal that your body is rising to push, and do it again.

There's no multitasking during this stage! Although some women are chatty during the short periods of rest between pushes (especially at the beginning), others are serious, quiet, and often very tired. But when you are pushing, your concentration is right there and only there. I remember during one birth I came out of a wave of pushing to realize the whole birthing team (about six people) was yelling my name at me, trying to get my attention. Despite the fact that they were only three feet away, *I didn't hear them*. It's *that* kind of focus.

This is cooperating with God's work. All your attention, right here, right now. Too often we live scattered lives, unable to focus on what's important—but not now. Go ahead and push with God. He wants this baby to be born, and this birth to be completed. He wants you to experience that baby in your arms. Put aside any other concern and yield to the Spirit's work in this stage.

Crowning and self-doubt

The final part of the pushing stage may be marked by the sign of self-doubt (again). Maybe this pushing stage has been much more painful that you expected. Or maybe it has gone well, but the exhaustion of the work is catching up fast. Or you are experiencing "crowning"—when the baby's head is stretching out the vaginal opening and not slipping back in the birth canal. While the pressure of the baby's head will act as a natural anesthetic, the initial stretching presents a stinging sensation for a little bit (some call it the "ring of fire") that is, at best, odd. Your midwife or doctor will also tell you to stop trying to push, since too much pressure at this point could cause tearing. It makes sense but is hard to do when your whole body wants to push!

The biggest antidote to self-doubt is the closeness of the baby. The medical team will often encourage the mother to feel the baby's head or show her in a mirror what is happening. The other antidote is to remember the presence of the Holy Spirit in this place. Keep breathing through all this: breathe in the Holy Spirit, breathe out your doubts. Keep breathing.

"Let birth happen? I'm working hard here!"

One of the things that you may hear from doctors and midwives at the end of this pushing stage is to "let birth happen." And it makes sense: the crowning and birthing of the baby happen of their own accord. You don't say, "Okay, body, crown!" And the attendants want to help ease the child out if necessary. But it can be *very hard work* to let birth happen.

There is a spiritual component to this. In all of life, we need to allow God to transform us, heal us, make us saints. Our role is to be open to God, to trust, and let God work. Our role is to know that we are not in the driver's seat here. God is. Trust that. But it will be hard. Most things worth doing are hard.

On the other hand, there are few moments in life that are more moving or exciting, not just for you, but for everyone present. You have been given a birth, and have cooperated in bringing a child to new life. You have given your body in love to this child for months, and especially now. You may not savor the birth of your child at the time. But savor it soon: savor what is being accomplished through God's initiative.

For prayerful reflection

> This will sound almost heretical, but the phrase, "This is my body, given up for you," was very comforting during the worst of it. . . . It's all I could think of on my last one.
> — Christie Martin

That comment is not heretical at all, unless you have mistaken yourself for God. We are called to imitate Christ, and when birth is difficult, this is as close to the cross as many will approach. Perhaps you could consider praying with this Scripture beforehand. Whether the pushing stage (or the entire birth) is difficult or relatively easy is not entirely in your hands. But the truth that you are giving your body in love for another is never more concretely lived out than in giving birth. Pray with this Scripture beforehand, and consider the following statement from another Catholic mother:

> I have somehow likened it [pushing the baby out] to the effort needed to spread the truth of the Gospel. Always an effort, sometimes painful, and seldom unproductive. It is the uniquely feminine way of participating in God's creation.
> —Jaye

14

Receiving the Child

> With my first, I was exhausted. No one handed him to me until he was just about to be taken to the nursery. At that point a nurse called out, "Mum hasn't seen him yet!" I do have recollections of my husband carrying him around the delivery room singing, "Happy birthday to you. . . ." For the other children, I got them right away. It was always a treat to snuggle with the tiny, squishy little one and look into their seemingly bottomless eyes.
> —Jaye

This is a reflection that perhaps doesn't need words, and words that come do not touch what happens. Yes, the mother delivers the placenta, which in most Western cultures, is an afterthought.[46] But for most women, this is the moment when you first see and hold your child.

Cradling the child

If the baby and mother don't require special medical attention, there is usually an effort to let them bond. The baby may be put on the mother's body, skin to skin, which helps regulate the baby's breathing and temperature. They may be covered with a blanket for warmth and spend time cuddling, or nursing. The smell of the mother is familiar to the child, as is her voice. Sometimes lights are dimmed for baby's new eyes and the mother and father and child are left alone to have time to meet each other and recover from the birth.

It is a moment of genuine tenderness. *Tenderness* was a word highly valued by John Paul II:

> It is especially in relationships between two human beings that one of them is able to, and feels the need to, enter into the feelings, the inner state, the whole spiritual life of the other—and is able and needs to make the other aware of this.[47]
>
> . . .
>
> Tenderness is the ability to feel with and for the whole person, to feel even most deeply hidden spiritual tremors, and always to have in mind the true good of that person.[48]

Many women are full of mixed emotions at birth: relief, concern, joy. But seeing and holding the baby evokes tenderness, which is more than an emotion—it is a kind of love. The hospitality you offered the child in the womb has changed venues: you are introducing him to family, to the world.

Babies, especially in medically uncomplicated births, do not always come out distressed. But there is so much that is new—the light, the air, the cold, the unmuffled noise. Most women, if at all possible, want to take the child and protect her from that confusing newness. Most women hold the baby close, gaze intently, and say words like, "Hello, little baby. You are so beautiful. I am your mama. Shhh, it's okay, it's okay. I love you."

This natural impulse to set the baby in relationship is an act of tenderness. Those typical first words to the baby are an expression of what John Paul II wrote; the mother is "enter[ing] into the feelings, the inner state, the whole spiritual life of the other—and is able and needs to make the other aware of this."

The state of quiet awareness

Another event that typically occurs after a few moments of calming and quiet cuddling is the "look of quiet alertness." Don't miss this by reaching for your phone as soon as baby is cradled in your arms—the world can wait.

This is a moment for gazing, that long, loving beholding that we practiced in chapter 4. Give the baby your eyes and attention. Typically, baby's eyes will wander a bit until he focuses on the mother's eyes looking back at him. Newborns cannot see well, but can see perfectly within 10–12 inches—the exact distance of a nursing child's eyes to his mother's eyes. Within a half hour, a baby born through an unmedicated childbirth will enter this stage of quiet alertness and receive the world around him. (The baby also will fall into the quiet alertness stage off and on for the first few weeks of life.)

This time is a precious opportunity to practice the Law of the Gift, the giving and receiving that is the hallmark of the spiritual life. Baby is all about receiving as he takes it all in: learning who he is, learning who loves him. The mother responds by giving that love, that knowledge of who he is, that security. But she also has the opportunity to receive: the gift that is the child, the gift of new relationship, the gift of her vocation to motherhood.

Nursing

Some women have difficulty with nursing, some do not want to nurse, and others are unable to nurse at all (for example, if they are on medications that can harm the baby). However, if you are able, I would encourage you to nurse the baby for at least the first few days, or even just the first day. The first few days, women produce colostrum, a kind of "supermilk" that is incredibly advantageous to the baby. The regular milk that comes in later is remarkably advantageous, too. I personally found nursing to be very healing after a difficult first birthing experience. It does take some practice, so connecting with a lactation consultant or the La Leche League could be helpful. In any case, there are probably few greater symbols of giving and receiving than the nursing mother and child.

When the mother nurses, she gives of herself to address her baby's basic need of hunger. She satisfies baby's hunger and even boosts his immune system. She also addresses very naturally his need to be touched, cuddled, and loved. Nursing may even involve sacrifice (those 3 AM feedings and more).

And what is received? The opportunity to connect, emotionally and physically, with your baby; a happy, healthier baby; and (unless you are having unusual difficulties) a pleasant and relaxing feeling. Nursing was designed to nourish your child, nutritionally and emotionally. If you do not or cannot nurse, many of these bonding elements can be incorporated into bottle feeding (holding close, skin to skin, cooing and connecting).

But what if . . . ?

But what if none of this goes according to plan? What if you are too exhausted to connect with your baby? What if your baby has medical issues that require immediate help? What if you can't nurse?

The way mothers receive their child after birth was designed by God to provide many gifts to both mother and child. But those gifts are not absolutely necessary. God is all-powerful and creative, and we may receive our sign that we are called to motherhood in different ways. You may need to find or help create these graced moments with your child. And that is okay. As I said, we live in a fallen world. We're birdwatchers on the lookout for signs of grace.

When I gave birth to my first child, I had a C-section after forty-seven hours of labor. I had a spinal block and was strapped to a surgical bed, and after they tugged my son out, they rushed him, crying, to the pediatric table to check things out. He was fine. I, on the other hand, was experiencing a massive headache and nausea from the anesthesia and still couldn't move my arms (which were strapped down). Someone suggested I hold the baby, but I couldn't see how and thought I was going to throw up. He was still crying. So my husband held the baby close to me, and I sang a song that I had sung to him every day while he was in the womb. He immediately quieted down, listening alertly.

That was a true moment of grace. He knew me and I knew him. He stayed with my husband while I recovered from surgery and the previous forty-seven hours. Our first meeting should have been better . . . but what was given was enough.

For prayerful reflection

> Yet it was you who took me from the womb; you kept me safe on my mother's breast.
>
> On you I was cast from my birth, and since my mother bore me you have been my God.
> —Psalm 22:9–10
>
> If it is not clear, the "you" in this psalm is God.

Consider praying this Scripture through *lectio divina*, beginning by deliberately placing yourself in the light of Christ:

> *Read/listen*: Read the Scripture aloud, slowly and deliberately, at least three times. Continue reading them aloud or silently as inspired. Linger on words that move you.
>
> *Meditate on the words*: What strikes you about this passage? Do any words or phrases seem to rise to the top? You may want to look at all of Psalm 22 in order to have more context for these words.

Dialogue with God: Speak with the Lord about this passage. Give your questions and emotions to the Holy Spirit, and ask for light; ask the Lord what he wants you to know.

Contemplate and rest: Take some time to rest in God's presence. As the scripture says, "On you I was cast from my birth . . . ." Perhaps this is an image to guide your contemplation and rest in the providence of God.

Lectio divina, by the way, is an ancient Christian prayer practice that translates literally as "sacred reading." If you find this reflection exercise helpful, you may wish to look for more in-depth resources on this practice.

15

Last Thoughts on Giving Birth

At least two potential dangers face you in reading Part II of this book.

One is that you have not given birth, and now have set in your mind what your birth will look like, down to the details. You have an ornately framed picture in your head of the perfect birth. This can be spiritually fatal because the perfectly patterned birth is only a figment of the imagination. Worse, you could spend your entire birthing experience comparing your real birth to your imagined perfect birth.

Remember Ignatius's first foundation:

> . . . We should not fix our desires on health or sickness,
> wealth or poverty, success or failure, a long life or short one.
> For everything has the potential of calling forth in us
> a deeper response to our life in God.
>
> Our only desire and our one choice should be this:
> I want and I choose what better
> leads to the deepening of God's life in me.[49]

There is a lot going on every time you give birth. These chapters are meant to be a help in recognizing that God wants to draw you to himself by giving you signs of grace and love within the process of gestation and birth. If the birth begins to go in a direction that you do not expect, look for God, lean on God, and remember (perhaps afterward) that everything has the potential of calling forth in us a deeper response to our life in God.

When I was typing this book, at one point I meant to type "Be the birdwatcher," and accidentally typed "Be the birthwatcher." But slip of the fingers or not, this is what you are called to do, during birthing if you can, or afterward as you process the landscape of your birthing experience. Signs are meant to lead us in the right direction. Birth can be the sign that leads us to a fuller relationship with God. But put away any specific expectations about what the birth will look like. It could be very different from what you expect.

The second potential danger is that you have already given birth, and are reading this book to process your birth. You are struggling because your birth did not look like what is described here; instead, you were miserable, or disappointed, or even abused.

I am deeply sorry, and all I can say is at least one of my births fit that category, even as I absolutely loved the child we received. You are not alone in this; in fact, it is quite common. But our God is a God of healing. The next chapters are for you.

When Childbearing Is Difficult, Where Is God?

16

Difficulty Conceiving: He Heals the Brokenhearted

It's been four months, eight months, a year or more. Your good-hearted friends and family are making light jokes about it being time to start a family. And you don't have the heart to tell them you've been trying and nothing seems to be happening.

Fertility challenges are incredibly common. Six percent of married women in the US ages 15–44 are infertile, and almost another 11 percent have impaired fertility.[50] The monthly grind of charting ovulation, waiting, then . . . no pregnancy . . . can be very wearing.

There are many resources to help women and men decide what happens next. Some advocate trying to boost the body's chances of conceiving naturally through nutrition and NFP; Marilyn M. Shannon's *Fertility, Cycles, and Nutrition* (Couple to Couple League, 4th ed., 2009) is one example. Others, such as Jean Dimech-Juchniewicz's *Facing Infertility: A Catholic Approach* (Pauline Books & Media, 2012), help couples wade through the medical options in an ethical and spiritual manner.

One important thing to remember is that you have no less of a sacramental marriage because you are struggling to conceive. Conception and parenthood is not an achievement, or a measure of success. Whether you are called to raise children or not is up to the Lord, who knows and loves you better than you do yourself. His plan for your life is, literally, glorious. Remember that.

Remember that Ignatius says that insofar as gifts lead us toward our goal ("to live with God forever"), they are good; but insofar as gifts lead us away from the goal that is life in God, they harm us. Try not to let your understandable desire for a child become the "first goal," replacing the ultimate goal of your life that is God. You can certainly pray for a child: God wants us to express the desires of our hearts. But also pray to grow closer to God above all things. And remember, "He heals the brokenhearted, and binds up their wounds" (Psalm 147:3).

In the Old Testament, we have many examples of God blessing his people through the gift of children. But you are blessed regardless. Your marriage is blessed. And God has a plan for your lives. It simply may not be the plan you expected, and may require more specific discernment.

The invitation to adoption

Couples who cannot conceive are not required, but invited, to consider adoption. Whether you are able to conceive naturally or not, you owe it to yourself to consider adopting a child. There are many children who need parents to love them. Consider adoption prayerfully, and ask God whether he may be leading you to be the answer to a child's prayer.

We adopted a child ourselves after having four biological children. While in my adopted son's birth country, my husband and I met another adopting couple who were adopting their fifth child. When I asked what led them to adopt these children, the mother said that a few years into their marriage, they had come to terms with the fact that "God had closed the womb." I was struck by that phrase, and her demeanor: a little sad, but mostly at peace.

She continued: "I didn't realize then what a blessing it would be to be able to adopt these children. We wanted children to love, they wanted parents. God brought goodness out of tragedy, and I know we were called to do this. It has been the biggest blessing of our lives." Most of the children she and her husband adopted have special needs and would have had a hard time getting adopted otherwise. Adoption can be difficult, and it is perhaps not for everyone. But it can often be a powerful way to love, to parent, to grow closer to God's heart.

Hope

Where there is God, there is healing and life. How God wants you to live out your vocation may not be clear to you now but his love for you and your husband never wavers. Make a conscious decision to live in hope that God will unfold the path you are given to walk, and know he walks it with you. Hope is a decision, as well as the antidote to despair and anxiety.

I close with a definition of hope I love, from a friend:

> . . . Hope is not as sweet and cute as it sounds, as if it is a pretty fluttering butterfly trying to get out of a netted jar. I see hope as much more of a persistent and determined spirit. More like the Holy Spirit. . . . Hope presses through all, not sweetly and gently, but firmly, with a power that does not let go.
> —Fran Rossi Szpylczyn

For prayerful reflection

1. Pray with these two scriptures. What do they say to you, as you struggle with whether you are called to bear a biological child or not?

> For surely I know the plans I have for you, says the Lord, plans for your welfare and not for harm, to give you a future with hope. Then when you call upon me and come and pray to me, I will hear you. When you search for me, you will find me; if you seek me with all your heart, I will let you find me, says the Lord, and I will restore your

fortunes and gather you from all the nations and all the places where I have driven you, says the Lord, and I will bring you back. . . .
—Jeremiah 29:11–14

As a deer longs for flowing streams,
 so my soul longs for you, O God.
My soul thirsts for God,
 for the living God.
When shall I come and behold
 the face of God?
My tears have been my food
 day and night,
while people say to me continually,
 "Where is your God?"

These things I remember,
 as I pour out my soul:
how I went with the throng,
 and led them in procession to the house of God,
with glad shouts and songs of thanksgiving,
 a multitude keeping festival.
Why are you cast down, O my soul,
 and why are you disquieted within me?
Hope in God; for I shall again praise him,
 my help and my God.
—Psalm 42:1–6

2. In the Old Testament, Hannah pleaded in prayer for a child (1 Samuel 1:1–20). There is precedent if you wish to pray this way! But you could also ask the saints to intercede before God for the conception of a child. Some saints frequently called upon are St. Elizabeth (mother of John the Baptist and surprised by motherhood in older age after many years of not conceiving), St. John Paul II (who bears a deep love for families), St. Gianna Molla (who bore her last child under severe medical

circumstances that eventually ended her life), and St. Rita of Cascia (a patron of impossible causes, especially those dealing with sterility). There are others as well. Do some research and reach out to the saints, asking them to pray to God with you.

17

The Unexpected Child: Dealing with Shock, Fear, and Anxiety

No one wants to admit they were surprised by a pregnancy—not unless it's of the "Oh, what a pleasant surprise!" variety.

Sometimes we are just jarred: "Wow, I didn't expect that! I had other plans for the upcoming year!" And other times, it is more than jarring: Perhaps your family is in a financial crisis. Or dealing with a medical issue. Or struggling in our marriage or family life in one way or another.

A Catholic blogger and mother of eleven was heartbreakingly honest a week after announcing her unexpected pregnancy:

> . . . as kind and joyous as my readers seem to be, I am not. I've rewritten that sentence and deleted it three times because it seems like such an awful thing to say out loud, and yet it's the truth. The night that I found out I was pregnant again, I sat on the floor of my kitchen and silently sobbed for hours. This wasn't just bad news, it was devastating. Of all the things I've ever wanted in my life, I've never wanted anything more than I wanted to be not pregnant in that moment. The thought of it still brings tears to my eyes that well up and threaten to spill over.[51]

She went on to say that she had scheduled a hysterectomy for ongoing health issues (not life and death, but serious enough) just prior to receiving this news. It seemed to be time. But instead she ended with, "sometimes God calls you on your beliefs and asks you to put your money where your mouth is, and that's when you find out what it is that you really believe."

If you are experiencing an unexpected pregnancy, you may remember the promise that you made at your wedding (assuming you were married in the Catholic Church) to "accept children lovingly from God." And at some level you want to do just that . . . if only some of your emotions and circumstances didn't seem to be standing in the way.

Dealing with circumstances

This brief reflection can't begin to cover all of the circumstances you might be facing. But try to think creatively and proactively. If something is in the way, what can be changed? If money is an issue, be active about seeking help (in paying the hospital bill, seeing if you qualify for state assistance, perhaps taking on some extra work or different work for a while). Don't be ashamed to ask for help. You are taking care of your family as best you can. On the other hand, if your finances are okay, just not perfect, you may be invited to adjust your perspective. The car may last a couple more years just fine. The kids may be sleeping three to a bedroom for a bit.

Discuss health issues with your doctor. I will warn you that doctors commonly advise abortion for complicated medical conditions across the board, even when the issue is fairly minor. But we do live in a world with the most sophisticated medical care known since the dawn of civilization, and your doctors might help you see possibilities you didn't know about. Don't lose hope, be honest with your doctors, and give it to God.

Struggles in your marriage or family life can be hard—but also an opportunity to improve the situation. Consider getting an outside perspective from a counselor or a pastoral minister. Check out the Teams of Our Lady apostolate and Marriage Encounter as ways of strengthening your marriage, or Retrouvaille, if your marriage is more troubled.

Whatever your circumstances may be, take heart, take it to your support community, and take it to God. You are not alone, and there are people who want to help.

Dealing with emotions

Your emotions may be harder to address than your concrete circumstances. But they are real and should not be dismissed as frivolous. Talking through your feelings with a spiritual director or a trusted friend is ideal, but at minimum, offer your emotions to God.

If you are shocked, be shocked. That will wear off with time; you have about nine months to get used to this new little person and reality. Being surprised is no sin and can help you remember that God has plans that you do not even know about.

If you are afraid, do you know why you are afraid? Is there anything you can do to address that fear? Can you ask God for peace? Can you try to pray in peace?

Anxiety is a close relative to fear: it is basically worry that has gone into overdrive. Try to discern what is making you anxious. Is your anxiety an ongoing issue that needs medical treatment, or attention through counseling? What does it mean to hand that anxiety over to God?

If you are sad, be honest about what you may be losing, which is probably the cause of the sadness. Maybe the physical difficulty of the pregnancy itself, if you've had rough pregnancies, is causing the sadness: who wants months of bed rest? No one. Maybe you had other hopes in your life that need to be put aside for a while. Maybe it is something deeper and more serious than either of those.

Whatever it is, be honest, and bring it to God. God knows about your troubles already, but until you tell him, you are not offering an opening for him to work in your life. Only God knows our futures. But we know God wants our happiness in this world and the next. Ask him to show you the goodness, and to apply balm to the sadness. If the sadness moves into something more serious, such as depression, continue praying but also consult a counselor or doctor.

What is love, anyway?

Part of accepting children lovingly from God means to love the child. Most women at one point or another are gifted with an emotionally intense love for their children. But often it isn't the first day they find out they are pregnant! Regardless of emotions, love is practiced and honored when you take care of yourself (which includes the baby) by eating healthy, getting exercise as you can, and resting. Love is practiced when you put your hand gently on your expanding midsection. Love is practiced when you talk to the baby. Love is practiced when you pray for the baby, yourself, and the birth.

Any love you give the baby comes from God and is the work of God. He will help you love this child if you cooperate with his will. Breathe, pray, ask for peace, and look for ways to love this child.

For prayerful reflection

I suggested above to pray for peace, whatever the situation. Do more than ask for peace, though. Pray to be reminded that God *is* peace, and God holds you close. A well-known Scripture comes to mind:

> The Lord is my shepherd, I shall not want.
> He makes me lie down in green pastures;
> he leads me beside still waters;
> he restores my soul.
> He leads me in right paths for his name's sake.
>
> Even though I walk through the darkest valley,
> I fear no evil; for you are with me;

your rod and your staff—
they comfort me.

You prepare a table before me
in the presence of my enemies;
you anoint my head with oil; my cup overflows.
Surely goodness and mercy shall follow me
all the days of my life,
and I shall dwell in the house of the Lord
my whole life long.
—Psalm 23

And St. Teresa of Avila penned a prayer, found tucked in her Bible after her death, that captures the eternal peace of God well—a peace that prevails over all circumstances:

Let nothing disturb you,
Let nothing frighten you,
All things are passing away:
God never changes.
Patience obtains all things
Whoever has God lacks nothing;
God alone suffices.

18

Miscarriage and Stillbirth: Grieving the Child Who Goes with God

Ten to 25 percent of all pregnancies end in miscarriage.[52] Many occur before the woman even realizes she is pregnant, and others mostly occur in her first trimester of pregnancy. But a miscarriage occurs any time the child dies before twenty weeks gestation. After that, if the child dies before or during birth, it is called a stillbirth.

Whatever we call it, most women dread any sign that they may be losing a child in the womb: sudden bleeding, intense cramping. Bear in mind that some women do have a bout of bleeding during pregnancy, and it does not result in miscarriage. Symptoms can be misinterpreted. But any sign that causes concern should be checked with a doctor or midwife.

The grief that comes with the loss of a child *in utero* can be intense. Grief is healthy and natural. It's true that not everyone responds this way: perhaps you had barely absorbed that you were pregnant, and the miscarriage ended a reality that you had not yet fully embraced. Or you may be going through trials in life that have made you more numb to what is happening than is typical. But the sorrow of miscarriage and stillbirth is normal, and underlines an important truth: human life is good, a gift from God, and its loss is worth mourning.

What can we do?

One of the difficulties with such a loss is the feeling of helplessness, the inability to "make it all better." But there are things you can do—at the time or later—that may help heal your heart and live out your vocation to motherhood, which does not end with the death of your child.

- You can name the child. In some miscarriages, you cannot know whether the child was a boy or girl, but regardless, you can name your child. Some people pray for a name; others use the name they had already settled upon; others name the child after a beloved saint.
- You can request that a priest, deacon, or a lay minister lead you and your family through the ritual blessing for the parents of a miscarried child.[53]
- If your child is stillborn, the *Order of Christian Funerals*[54] provides the possibility of a funeral liturgy; options include a Mass, a simpler service, and a graveside Rite of Committal. Contact your pastor for options. You can have a Catholic funeral for your stillborn child even though the child was not baptized.

As for the baptism question . . . many parents express concern that their child was not baptized, and what that could mean for the state of the child's soul. The *Catechism of the Catholic Church* is clear that we can rely on the mercy and trustworthy love of God:

> As regards *children who have died without Baptism*, the Church can only entrust them to the mercy of God, as she does in her funeral rites for them. Indeed the great mercy of God who desires that all men should be saved, and Jesus' tenderness toward children which caused him to say: "Let the children come to me, do not hinder them," allow us

> to hope that there is a way of salvation for children who have died without Baptism.[55]

Additionally, John Paul II wrote these words to mothers grieving the loss of aborted children, and they may well apply to any mother who has lost a child in the womb: "*You will come to understand that nothing is definitively lost . . .*" (*Evangelium Vitae* #99).

Healing for the mother

One of the hardest realities of the vocation to parenthood is recognizing, sooner or later, that you are a caretaker. It is an important, necessary, and beautiful role, but the child belongs to God, always. We are given the experience of directly parenting a child only for a short while.

If the key to the Theology of the Body literature is found in the dynamic of the gift, in recognizing that life is a gift and we are called to live according to the Law of the Gift, then the key to healing may be to recognize that we are called to place our emotions, our hopes, and ultimately, our children, in the direct care of God. This calls for an enormous act of trust. But the Holy Spirit is there to help you.

If you have access to support groups, friends, and family, by all means, lean on them in this time. But lean on God as well, in prayer. The prayer may be raw but it will be real, and that is what counts. The following reflection and prayer exercise is meant for women who have miscarried or suffered stillbirth. It is meant to be prayed as the woman feels ready (that is, perhaps not immediately, but soon). If the miscarriage was years ago, time stands still in the heart of God; pray it anyway.

For prayerful reflection

Thus says the Lord: A voice is heard in Ramah, lamentation

> and bitter weeping. Rachel is weeping for her children; she refuses to be comforted for her children, because they are no more. (Jeremiah 31:15)

Or perhaps you are not weeping. You are numb. Keeping busy. Trying to pretend today is normal.

Perhaps this was an unexpected pregnancy and the miscarriage only makes you more confused. How can a person feel sorrow and relief at the same time?

Whatever your reactions are, do two things:

1. First, acknowledge your feelings by taking them to God. Yes, God knows—but pretend God doesn't know what you are feeling, and describe every bit of it anyway. Recall the goodness of God and his promises. God is *not* the enemy who took your child; we live in a fallen world, and death is one of its bitter realities. Jesus Christ is the Divine Physician, the One who loves you and this child so completely that you cannot fully comprehend it. Place an act of trust in his love and mercy, and take your emotions to God, placing them in his hands.

If you cannot make that act of trust, ask God to help you trust him. Perhaps pray with this passage from Lamentations:

> [M]y soul is bereft of peace; I have forgotten what happiness is; so I say, "Gone is my glory, and all that I had hoped for from the Lord." . . . My soul continually thinks of it and is bowed down within me. But this I call to mind, and therefore I have hope: The steadfast love of the Lord never ceases, his mercies never come to an end; they are new every morning; great is your faithfulness. "The Lord is my portion," says my soul, "therefore I will hope in him." The Lord is good to those who wait for him, to the soul that seeks him. (3:17–25)

2. Second, realize this: you are *still* a mother to this child. Even if this is your first pregnancy, and you have no living children, you are *still* a mother. This vocation to motherhood is a gift and is never taken away. You can pray for this child, and ask the child to pray for you. That relationship is everlasting. All of us who bear children have to acknowledge, sooner or later, than we are caretakers: that children have been given to us for a time—days, weeks, years—and we are called to care for them in that time. But all of us are destined to go to God. All of us need to return the beautiful gift of a child to God's complete healing, nourishment, and care. The greatest and hardest mothering act we can do, after placing our grief or confusion or numbness in God's hands as an act of trust, is to place our children in his arms. You are not renouncing your motherhood, nor has it been taken away. You are fulfilling it. You are leading your child to God in the only way you can. Even if Jesus scooped up that child as he or she was failing and flooded him or her with a love of such intensity and beauty it cannot be described, your role in this amazing moment, the entry into God's love and light, is made complete when you yield your child to God. The role of mothers is to lead their children to God. Even though it is a tragedy whenever mother and child do not have much time together, the relationship is real and important, and as John Paul II said, never definitively lost.

If you are ready:

Go to a quiet place: your room, a chapel, an open field.

Ask the Holy Spirit to help you pray.

Then imagine yourself holding your child, and reflect on any details that come to mind.

Imagine Jesus next to you: what he looks like, the understanding in his eyes, how he considers you. Is he holding your hand? Sitting next to you?

If you have something to say, say it. You will know what to say.

Eventually—when the time feels right—hand over your child to Jesus. He takes your hand. Listen to him say, "You are always this child's mother."

You may even hear him say, "*Thank you.*"

19

A High-Risk Birth: Are Medical Interventions Clouding the Sign of Birth?

In the American medical system, certain realities in the health of the mother may lead the pregnancy and birth to be categorized as high risk. The woman may be very young or old. The woman may have a preexisting condition that requires special attention throughout pregnancy, such as diabetes or high blood pressure. If this is a second pregnancy, the pregnancy may be considered high risk based on how the previous labor and delivery went. Sometimes, the condition of the baby (or the number of babies in the womb) may make the pregnancy high risk. As you can see, high-risk pregnancy may sound ominous, but it is quite common, and some of the risks are more serious than others.

The bottom line is, medical professionals classify some pregnancies as high risk because they want to ensure the health of both the mother and the baby. These mothers are often referred to perinatologists for some or all of their care. In some cases, it is determined that the baby would be safest delivered early, or by a C-section.

If you have a high-risk pregnancy, with its attendant medical interventions, does this mean you will not be able to see the signs of birth? Not necessarily, but it will be different. Let's look at this in two ways. First, if you are anticipating giving birth with the "high risk" reality, let's see what you can do to preserve and honor some of the natural signs of birth. Secondly, if your birth is necessarily going to be very high-tech, let's look at how to adjust the welcoming of your child spiritually.

Honoring the spiritual signs of birth in a high-risk pregnancy

Even if your pregnancy is categorized as high risk, it is possible you may be able to have a natural vaginal birth, perhaps with some modifications. If this is your preference, tell your doctor, and ask questions. If he or she advises certain medical interventions, ask why they are needed. Such interventions might include continuous rather than intermittent fetal monitoring, or a heparin lock (in case you need intravenous medicine quickly), or a C-section that is scheduled before even trying labor and vaginal birth. Understanding *why* decisions are being made goes a long way toward feeling better about the course of the birth.

Once you know what is likely to occur, you can see what can be done to honor the spiritual nature of the event within those parameters. For instance:

- Will your husband be present?
- Will religious items (like a crucifix or rosary) be allowed into the room?
- You may not need to relax through contractions if you are having a scheduled C-section, but relaxing and entrusting the event to God may be even more important in a high-risk pregnancy. Think about how you can do that, before and during the birth.
- You may want a priest, or family and friends, to bless you and the baby before a medical intervention.
- Afterward, how many of the bonding protocols between mother and child can be retained? Will your husband be with your child, or with you?

- As much as you can, try to preserve the "high touch" nature of the event, and let the technology assist the birth rather than become the focus.[56] The technology is there to keep you and your child safe, period. The "drama" is the actual birth of your child.

Honoring a high-tech birth spiritually

The problem with a medically augmented birth is not the technology, which can be a lifesaver. But problems arise when those helping deliver the baby treat the mother and the child as objects rather than human beings. Respecting their humanity, their need to connect, and the inauguration of motherhood may get lost when the focus shifts to technological interventions. This can happen in a natural childbirth, too, but the shiny, blinking, beeping, attention-grabbing distraction that is medical technology seems to make the loss of the human touch more common in higher-tech births. Anything that the medical team can do to honor the bonding of the mother and child under the circumstances is a spiritual act of respect. For this reason, engaging a doula may make sense, as she can be an advocate for you. Your husband, too, can advocate for you.

But there is one Advocate above all others, and that is the Holy Spirit. Whatever happens, remember that the Holy Spirit is just as present at this birth as at any other birth. If you know your birth will be scheduled, perhaps you can take advantage of that by praying a novena to the Holy Spirit, ending on the day of the induction or C-section. Consider ways to remember that the Holy Spirit abides with us, even in the most unfamiliar places.

For prayerful reflection

Many religious women who are facing serious high-risk births are already praying, and praying hard. If you are having a high-risk birth, consider how to prepare yourself spiritually, and consider going to Reconciliation and Mass the day before. But the challenge will be to let go of your worst fears about the situation. Consider doing a bit of imaginative prayer with this Scripture from Isaiah 41:8–10:

> But you, Israel, my servant, Jacob, whom I have chosen, the offspring of Abraham, my friend; you whom I took from the ends of the earth, and called from its farthest corners, saying to you, "You are my servant, I have chosen you and not cast you off"; do not fear, for I am with you, do not be afraid, for I am your God; I will strengthen you, I will help you, I will uphold you with my victorious right hand.

The words here are God speaking through the prophet Isaiah to Israel, as Israel is on the cusp of possible destruction. Could you imagine God saying these words to you, substituting the word "Jacob" with your own name? Consider how God promises to be present to you in any time of trouble, including this one.

20

Postpartum Depression: When Contentment Cannot be Felt

> . . . I was completely unprepared for the anxiety disorder that accompanied my pregnancy hormone surge.
>
> I had always been a "worrier." But whatever worries or anxiety I had experienced before paled in comparison to the panic and fears that took over my barely pregnant body.
>
> When my son finally arrived, I was overcome with love. I adored him. But I couldn't stop crying. I couldn't sleep. I could barely force air into my lungs.
>
> . . . .
>
> [The nurses] all talked about their children and I remember staring at them wondering how they had survived becoming mothers and actually returned to the world.
>
> I couldn't imagine an hour without tears, let alone life as a working mother. I was sure I was destined to forever experience this fear and worry. I loved my new little baby too much. It was too much to bear. It was all just too much. Fortunately, a week later at my baby's check-up, the doctor immediately recognized my condition, and I began to get help for my anxiety and postpartum depression.[57]

Postpartum depression seems like the cruelest trick: after months of waiting and preparing for the new baby, swaddled in hope and love, you can't get out of bed. Life seems meaningless and you burst into tears at the drop of a hat. You're overwhelmed and can't function. This wasn't the way it was supposed to be, you think.

On top of that, no one else seems to think anything is other than lovely. "Oh, what a beautiful baby! Aren't they so sweet at this age? You must be so happy!"

Yet postpartum depression (PPD) is common—eight to 19 percent of new mothers report symptoms of PPD[58]—so it is good to be aware of it. While most women go through a short period called "the baby blues" a week or so after the baby is born, if you increasingly feel miserable, trapped, and emotionless, you may have crossed the line into PPD.

Risk factors for postpartum depression

If you have a history of depression, you are more likely to experience PPD. If you have had a stressful year for any number of reasons, that too is a risk factor. But even if you had a pleasant year and no history of depression, PPD can occur. The causes are various: the massive hormonal shifts that occur after birth, lack of sleep, the challenge of recovering after a C-section, and lifestyle changes (having a baby is almost always a lifestyle change!).

There are resources out there, and your medical team probably made you aware of them. It's hard to reach out when you are depressed and overwhelmed, but do it. You do not have to feel this way, and PPD is treatable.

Consider some of these ways to proactively head off PPD:

- Plan for extra help around the home for a few days or even weeks after the baby's birth.
- Lower your expectations for household cleanliness.
- Accept free meals from friends (indeed, hint that this may be welcomed more than knickknacks for the baby!).
- With the help of your husband or friends, try to schedule

time out of the house every day (even just a walk)—baby will be okay without you for a little while. Take that walk with baby in a stroller or carrier if you have to.

- Find a way to get sleep. Being sleep deprived never, ever helps.

These may sound like luxuries, but they aren't. The first few weeks are tough. Then it gets better. We used to live in cultures that supported childbirth through community and extended family efforts, and now, when many family members live far away from each other and we don't know our neighbors, we simply don't. It is a loss and makes the first weeks harder than they need to be.

But even with decent support, PPD happens. It is not a character flaw or something to be ashamed of; PPD is a disease, period. You would see someone to treat strep throat, so go see someone to treat depression! The very best thing you can do for yourself and your baby is to see a doctor or counselor. If you cannot see someone soon through scheduling, go to urgent care or even the ER. There are antidepressants that can help, and can be used with relative safety while nursing. Conversation therapy can be a real aid as well, and an antidote to feeling overwhelmed and alone.

Spiritually handling postpartum depression

Spiritually, depression is very difficult to deal with. The nature of the disease is that it can make you feel isolated and hopeless. PPD can sabotage any contentment you have in your new vocation. I would encourage readers with PPD to remember that the feelings are part of the disease and are, by definition, not accurate markers of the reality you are in. You feel worthless? You are not, that's PPD speaking. You feel like you are a bad mother? Once again, PPD talk. You feel like you will never be happy again? PPD, not reality. Many of the saints have said that while we must pay attention to feelings and where they are coming from, diseased emotions may fool you into thinking God is not your anchoring love. They may fool you into thinking you have been abandoned by Christ. Prayer of any sort that is honest and places some kind of trust in God is important. Having others pray for you is important. Praying with others, and letting them do most of the work of praying (because it is hard to pray when you are depressed), is important.

There are many saints who were depressed—and not just before a conversion experience, but also during their lives in the Church. St. Jane Frances de Chantal, St. Benedict Joseph Labre, St. Dymphna, St. Elizabeth Ann Seton, and St. Francis Xavier describe states that sound very much like depression, and there are many others as well. Asking them to intercede with God for your health and clear sight could be helpful.

Dom John Chapman, OSB, rather famously said, "Pray as you can, not as you can't." Wise words, especially for those who are exhausted and depressed. If you are depressed, ask for concrete help, see a doctor, and ask friends and families for prayers. In the meantime, consider praying the prayer below, or adapting it to your situation.

For prayerful reflection

Consider speaking to God honestly through this prayer, or one of your own creation:

> Dear God,
>
> I don't want to get up.
>
> I feel overwhelmed.
>
> I feel like I want things to go back to the way things were: Baby in the womb, meals at regular times, going out with

friends . . . just what was normal.

I can't figure out nursing, or sleeping, or anything.

I'm up all night by myself with a crying baby and feel like I can't make it better.

It feels like this is never going to get better; that being a mother to your child will never get easier.

I don't want to get up, but I want to run away, too.

I just want to cry.

As the blind beggar said, "Jesus, Son of David, have mercy on me."[59]

Heal me of this depression.

Help me to remember that this time is temporary.

Help me to remember that this child was meant for me, to bring me happiness.

Help me to love, even when my brain seems to be blocking the way.

Help me to feel the care of people around me.

Help me to feel your love and peace.

Help me find the help I need today; help others find me.

Son of David, have pity on me and heal me.

Jesus, I trust in you.

Jesus, I trust in you.

Jesus, I trust in you.

I beg you, weave your Holy Spirit, the Consoler, around me and the baby like a ribbon of love and light.

Jesus, help me to trust in you.

Seeking the Holy Spirit in Birth Stories

I was privileged to interview a number of Christian women who shared their birth stories with me for this book. I have chosen stories that span a wide range of birth experiences to demonstrate the many ways the Holy Spirit is embraced in birth.

As you read these stories, consider the three spiritual keys: give God permission to work in your life and relax into openness; cooperate with God's intention to realize your motherhood through your body now; and yield to the work of the Holy Spirit. Consider how each woman attended to those keys during her birthing experience.

21

JoAnna: "God Was Present Throughout"

JoAnna Wahlund lives in Arizona and is a Catholic mother of seven, including two miscarried children. This story focuses on the birth of her fourth child, Gabriel.

I had my fourth child on November 26, 2011. Two days before his birth I cooked Thanksgiving dinner for nine people, and I think that's what sent me into labor. The next day, November 25, I was exactly full term (thirty-seven weeks). The day started with some spotting, and in the late afternoon I started having mild but regular contractions. The contractions continued throughout the evening and into the night. We went to the hospital around midnight. When we arrived, I was only 4 cm so my husband, doula, and I walked around for an hour or two. When we went back to the L & D ward, [they determined] I had made progress so they admitted me. I labored in the Jacuzzi tub for a while, and started feeling like I had to push around 5 AM. I was only at 7 cm so I sat on a birth ball for a while [to help dilation progress]. Eventually I got restless and started pacing the room, stopping to lean over the bed with each contraction. At 6 AM, my body started pushing involuntarily and part of the amniotic fluid sac came out while I was standing at the end of the bed. I climbed into the bed on my hands and knees while the nurses called the doctor. He came quickly, and the baby was born in two or three pushes. The amniotic sac didn't break until his shoulders were born. Gabriel Keith weighed 7 lbs, 9 oz.

Did you use any particular childbirth method, or did you have opinions going in about how to best give birth?

Before my first child was born, my husband and I had studied the Bradley Method of natural childbirth. We never took a formal class in the Bradley Method, but we read everything we could get our hands on about natural childbirth, and we took a Lamaze class that our local hospital offered. I was determined to give birth without pain medication of any kind, and I've achieved that goal with every birth so far. I didn't want the cascade of interventions that can happen in a very medically managed birth.

Did you engage in any spiritual practices prior to birth? Can you describe them?

I prayed often to St. Gerard [the patron saint of difficult childbirths], asking for a safe delivery. I had a holy card with a prayer to St. Gerard for a safe delivery and I said [the prayer] often. I also used visualization techniques—I visualized what my idea of a "perfect" birth would be, and asked God for help to make it happen. Above all, though, I was praying that both the baby and I would come through the delivery safely, even if interventions were necessary.

Did you engage in any spiritual practices during your birth?

While I was walking the halls of the hospital during labor, we stopped by the hospital chapel and prayed there. It was around 2 AM, so it was very quiet and peaceful. I also said the Divine

Mercy prayer while having contractions. I would inhale slowly and deeply while praying silently, "For the sake of your sorrowful passion . . ." and then exhale slowly while praying silently, "Have mercy on us and on the whole world." I also concentrated on offering up the pain of my contractions for all infertile women who longed for a child, especially for a few personal friends of mine who were struggling with infertility. During transition it was hard to focus on longer prayers, so I was mainly praying, "O God, O God, have mercy on me," and "Mary, help me." And right after he was born, I said an immediate prayer of thanksgiving, just a "Thank you, God!"

In retrospect, where was God in your birthing process? Was there a place where you sensed the presence of the Holy Spirit? Or Mary?

God was present throughout. I definitely felt the Holy Spirit as I was laboring in the tub. My doula had placed gauze pads soaked in clary sage essential oil around the tub, and breathing in the scent was reminiscent of smelling incense at Mass, which aided in my prayers. And I was reminded strongly of Mary when my baby boy was placed in my arms, because I felt like my joy mirrored her joy at the birth of Jesus (albeit in a lesser way, because nothing can compare to giving birth to the Savior of the world!).

Is there anything else you would like to add?

The times in my life when I have felt closest to God were immediately following childbirth, when my new child has been placed in my arms. The experience always magnifies my awe and wonder at the miracle of creation, and I feel so humbled that God allows [us] to participate in the creation of a new soul.

JoAnna's story of openness, cooperation, and yielding is a good example of a woman leaning on many elements in her spirituality, including a devotion to Mary and to the Chaplet of Divine Mercy. She made significant efforts to be prepared for the work of labor, as well as creating an environment that reminded her and others that God was present. Finally, her child's birth was graced with the gift of joy, a sign of the Holy Spirit.

22

Carla: *"I'm Going to Feel This Birth"*

Carla and her husband, Paul, are the parents of nine children, in addition to one who passed away at age two, and three children who were miscarried. They preferred to go by their first names only. They live in Illinois, and this interview begins with talking about the birth of their second child. It ends with her reflection on a hard-fought internal struggle to be open to having more children, only to miscarry twins, and how that affected her relationship with God.

For my second birth, with my son Luke, I barely made it to the hospital. My water broke in the car. I had had an hour and a half of labor. Driving, my water broke, my husband insisted on stopping for stop lights . . . we were living in Maryland then and were going to the National Naval Medical Center. He dropped me off at the emergency room and then went to *park the car* (laughing) . . . so I'm carrying this big pillow with me in front of me, you know, for the long labor I was supposed to have? Avoiding those uncomfortable hospital pillows? (more laughter) I lean over the triage desk with that pillow in front of me and I think the lady couldn't see I was nine months pregnant . . . and she says so sweetly, "Hello, can I help you?" I said, very deliberately, "I am going to have a baby *now*." And she said, "Oh, let's get you up to the seventh floor," and I said, "Nope, not going to happen!"

They walked me to a Cardiac Care room, with a slab and a bunch of things, and then called down a wench of an OB, who immediately said, "Oh, you couldn't get her upstairs? This is such a pain." She was really annoyed. Then someone starts getting ready to put in an IV and my husband says, "Oh please, do you think she's going to dehydrate in five minutes?" So she backed off of that. . . . So once Paul was there and I felt settled enough, I wanted to push. Then the OB shouted, "Wait, I've got to look at you before you can push!" And then she looked and said, "Oh yeah, you're all dilated. Fine, push, whatever." Literally, she was ticked off the whole time.

So I am getting ready to push and she says, "Yeah, the head's right there." So I half sat up to reach and feel the baby's head—I wanted to touch his head—and she *slapped my hand away.*

And she's like "Get your hand out of there! I can't see what's going on!" And . . . I thought, *Then if I can't feel him with my hands, I'm going to feel him as I give birth to him.* And . . . Paul was there, I felt safe, I knew the baby was coming, so I closed my eyes, and as I pushed, I said, "I want to feel him." And I literally felt *every contour* of his head. The rotation. The shoulders. The belly. The narrowness of the hips. His little feet coming out. I felt *every bit* of that. . . . That was a very powerful, even spiritual, way of knowing this child. That feeling as he came out (because it was basically one big push)—it was not specifically religious faith . . . but . . . the physical sensation of birthing his body made me feel intensely close to him spiritually and emotionally. And this was very different from my first child.

. . . Now I thought that doctor was a wench and maybe she was, but I turned that around into something that made me focus, focus beyond the difficulties of the physical sensations ("oh, this hurts, oh, this burns") and it became "I'm going to *feel* this." And that made me feel very connected to him very quickly.

I never experienced that with my other births. But that made me think of that connection between the physical and spiritual.

Do you think that move to deliberately "feel his birth" was inspired? You know, that it came from beyond . . . ?

It was. It helped that I felt very protected. Even though this [OB] was being a pain, I knew she wasn't in charge. I knew she wasn't in charge of me, my baby, my birth. . . . So yes, it was definitely not a conscious thing on my part. . . . I was in a good place emotionally in many ways, and had a lot of support for giving birth . . . [that internal prompt to deliberately feel the birth] made something that could have been really bad into something amazing.

It sounds like you weren't afraid during that birth. A lot of women talk about fear.

No, no, I was not. Even though there were a lot of things in the background. There was something else—I had been told that 99 percent of the women who use this hospital get epidurals. . . . I had been told if you don't want an epidural, then come in here *just before* you give birth. Well, I didn't plan it that way, but maybe subconsciously . . . boom! You're having an hour and a half labor and delivery. Really, there was no time to do anything. Maybe I turned that situation into a plus!

Later, after her husband fought and survived cancer, and they had settled into being a two career couple with two sons and a post-chemotherapy "miracle daughter". . . .

You know, the world was telling me [to stop having children], you have two boys and a girl, you have good work making a crud load of money, and I had twenty months of breastfeeding amenorrhea. . . . Then we started doing NFP. . . .

After a hard year of misunderstandings—he thought she didn't want more children, and she thought he didn't want more children—they decided they both really wanted another baby, if they could.

Well, I immediately got pregnant, so everything's okay, right? Wrong. Miscarriage, ovarian cyst, they thought they were twins . . . they prepared me for a D and C, and then, at the hospital just beforehand, they found a heartbeat. Oh dear God . . . sent home, hCGs started going up, hCGs starting going down. I was *not* going in for a D and C at that point, I said; this is going to happen when it is going to happen. So it was three weeks from the initial D and C hospitalization until I miscarried, in my bathroom. And I went to God: *I thought you wanted us to do this! We worked to get* our *will in line with* your *will and* then *you did this to me?*

And it was at this point I had a really, really deep reconversion experience. I had to decide whether redemptive suffering was real—or it wasn't. That to me was the linchpin. It makes no sense to the world, what I went through those weeks. But if redemptive suffering is real, and I'm sharing in the redemptive suffering of Christ, and it helped save me or another person halfway across the world, or my family or my husband or my children—that's *real.* Pain can be real and it means something and it is not to be avoided. I *really* deeply embraced that concept of redemptive suffering. And that helped me flow with my whole Catholic faith in a whole different way. I got pregnant with Ella right away afterward . . . all my next three births were super easy . . . not necessarily pain-free! But just with that sense of "I'm on board with God's will for this pregnancy, with this labor, with getting pregnant again"—whatever it is.

I feel like in our last birth, everything came together. The trust in God, the being in a safe and secure place, Paul's and my relationship—I feel those are the graces of the sacrament of matrimony, just flowing forth. [Realizing that] was a huge thing for me. Everyone thought we were crazy, having all these kids, and oh, you're almost 42?! . . . but we were taking our faith seriously, and just kept asking, what's the next step?

Carla and her husband went on to adopt four more children.

Carla's story is a great example of not being afraid, but yielding to the work of the Holy Spirit. The Holy Spirit, in turn, inspired a way out of a very bad birth setup with her second child and provided insight into the challenges of being open to more children, and the passion that followed her complicated miscarriage. Reading through her process of being open to new life is also a good reminder that childbirth and married life help you grow in your faith and relationship to God.

23

Leah: "God Is All Over Body and Birth for Me"

Leah Perrault is a Catholic pastoral minister and writer in Western Canada. She is married and has three children, and this story is about the recent birth of her third child, Charlize.

My water broke with my third baby on a Friday night. Labor started and stopped all weekend, with my older two kids away with Grandma and Grandpa. We had a midwife, who encouraged us to try to get labor going on its own rather than being induced if possible. The risk of infection goes up considerably after the third day (past water breaking). So by the time Monday morning came, I was feeling totally defeated, having walked and tried castor oil and homeopathics. . . . As a last-ditch effort to avoid medical induction and a hospital birth, we called an acupuncturist. As I lay on the table, still, letting the little needles do their work, I remember telling God I felt so defeated, but feeling a deep assurance that I wasn't, that he wasn't. Tears were rolling down my face as I made peace with my inability to make labor go, and then the contractions started, about 9:30, and didn't stop until Charlize was born at 4:04 that Monday afternoon, at home in our living room. It was my hardest labor, with the contractions coming every two minutes for most of the day, and by 11:30 convincing the midwives that birth was imminent . . . though more than four hours followed. I turn inward during labor, focused on the moment, trying to receive rather than resist the pain, relying on my husband to use his hands to relieve pressure on my hips and low back. This time, laughing gas was a total gift, and I used it for most of the contractions from 1:30 to 4:00.[60] It made the contractions blend together in my mind and took my focus off the time.

I love the end . . . the incredible pressure, the sure conviction that I can't do it, that I will fail, out of which comes the strength to push through the last millimeters of stretching that gives way to head and then shoulders, and then a cry. And the immediate relief of all the pain, baby passed into my arms, wet, and slippery and beautiful, comforted by being held.

Did you use any particular childbirth method, or did you have opinions going in about how to best give birth?

No methods, *per se*. I took prenatal classes with my first, which was a medically augmented labor lasting forty hours and including an epidural. It was a first try, a fumbling-in-the-dark labor and delivery that strengthened my desire for a midwife with the second. I think any birth that results in a live baby and mom is natural . . . but I wanted a birth that left me more connected with my body and its capacity, which is what I sought with babies two and three.

Did you engage in any spiritual practices prior to birth? Can you describe them?

I live a spiritual life, so it is hard to separate out the ones that are specific to birth. I pray for my kids, including in the womb, and before birth, ask God to help me to receive the labor and delivery as it goes, rather than trying to orchestrate it, which is futile anyway.

Did you engage in any spiritual practices during your birth?

Lots of people were praying for us through the pregnancy and I asked a handful of people to pray over the delivery weekend as it got more stressful. My spirituality is deeply embodied . . . I find it hard to give words to the ways that ordinary life is spiritually rich, especially in the midst of the experience.

A priest friend came and said Mass at the house on Sunday as labor was coming and going and getting to church was too much. It was a strange Mass, a ritual celebrating incarnation while incarnation was working itself in my body, richer in retrospect than in the moment, but a gift for sure.

In retrospect, where was God in your birthing process? Was there a place where you sensed the presence of the Holy Spirit? Or Mary?

God is all over body and birth for me, in the immediacy of the experience, in the intense focus that lets me do nothing other than the duty of the moment. God is in the pain and the relief, the presence of my husband and the midwives, in their encouragement and in the miracle of the baby.

Is there anything else you would like to add?

There is a pain for me in the theological reflection, too, in that the images of birth and birthing are so rich and so excluded from our teaching and preaching. . . . I'm looking forward to a time in our Church when these experiences are more freely shared and included in our reflection!

Leah's story is lovely for its emphasis on the presence of God in the entire process, which seems to help her express the intensity and beauty of the pushing process and the baby's emergence—not a process that everyone would describe as "beautiful to feel," but even in a challenging birth, she found it remarkable. Despite the difficulty of a near-stalled labor and sudden turnaround, she displays a significant openness to what God is doing in the moment.

24

Karen: "I Remember Praying Through the Pain in a New Way"

This mother wished to have her birth story interview published pseudonymously, so I am calling her Karen, and her son will be called James. Other names in the story also have been changed. She is a married mother of five children, and gave me this interview while in her third trimester with her fifth child.

Can you tell me a little bit about the actual birth experience? Where did it happen? Was it full term? How long was the labor? . . . The basic story?

This was James's birth, which was my third, and with my first two, once I got to the hospital I was in transition and it was like that (snaps fingers). So this was the first experience that I actually got time to prepare.

I was forty-one weeks, and it was the longest overdue I had gone. We had seen our midwife in the morning, and she said everything looked fine, and the fluids were fine and everything, so she gave us the option of breaking the water to get things going.

And . . . this is kind of interesting because the spirituality came in right away, because we walked down from our clinic visit and we saw Fr. Taylor. And we were just trying to be prayerful because she was putting this in our hands by saying, "You make the decision." And I was thinking that we're not *supposed* to make this decision, these things are supposed to just happen. . . . So we walk down and we saw [Fr. Taylor], and then another priest, waiting by the lab or something, and we just chatted with each of them, and asked for prayers.

We went to [a local restaurant] to have lunch, and we decided . . . to go ahead with it, so we went back to the Cathedral. . . . We were the only ones in the [adoration] chapel, but I just remember Tim and I having this wonderful prayer time together and just feeling like we're entering into this not knowing if it's right to get labor going ourselves, but feeling like it's time and everything will be okay. . . .

So we had a chance to kind of get everything laid out, I got to get my slippers on, and I had a St. Gerard holy card that someone lent me to carry during labor; I had that sitting by my bed. I was in no position to pray a rosary or anything like that. . . .

When [the midwife] broke my water she discovered that there was meconium [in the amniotic fluid]. . . . Knowing that my baby was swimming in this and I had read about the dangers of them inhaling it . . . it kind of heightened the anxiety level a little bit. . . .

I think she broke my water around 4 or 4:30 PM and then he was born at 10 PM that night. So it wasn't too long, but it was longer than either of my previous labors had been.

Did you use any sort of drugs or any sort of techniques to deal with the pain? Or did you just decide that "I'm bracing myself for pain and I'm going to do this"?

. . . [W]hen I was pregnant the first time I took a prenatal class that wasn't Bradley or anything specific, just talking about breathing and massage techniques, and stuff like that. But I didn't really remember anything like that, and I didn't prepare anything like that for that part of it.

But I remembered one of my friends had [asked her friends for their prayer requests] so she could bring [that list] with her to the hospital, so when she was in labor she could offer her pain as a prayer for whatever her friends wanted to pray for. . . .

That was a new concept for me that I had never really thought about . . . so I thought, oh, that's a great idea! I could do that, and it made so much sense to me: this is the most pain a woman probably goes through, and why not take that and offer it? . . .

I was able to get into the whirlpool, and I had never been able to before because I had never had the time, but I really liked having that little bit of preparation time. . . . Tim loves to sing and chant, and the acoustics in the bathroom were appealing to him, so we sang the Chaplet of Divine Mercy together. . . . It was very lovely and physically calming like prayer or like breathing can be, but it was also a reminder that this can be about more than just the pain that I'm experiencing right now.

So I came with a list . . . and I just kind of had [Tim] tell me the name of the person or give me an idea of who to pray for. And I remember one in particular was someone in my life that I don't really get along with that well . . . and I had him on my list, so I thought, "Oh, this is going to be a bad one!" (*laughs*) I don't remember if it was or not, but I just recall that was a big part, and I look forward to doing that again. . . .

I've found that after birth, the pains as you're nursing and the uterus contracting are so much worse.

Yes, it gets worse as you have more children.

Yes, I wish it would've gotten easier! . . . But I just took that as an opportunity to say, "I know this hurts so much, but I'm offering it up for him." And it was all kind of a prayer. . . . I just remember being alone there with him in pain and praying through that in a new way that I don't think I ever did in my first twenty-five to thirty years of life.

In the run-up to giving birth, in the days or weeks ahead of time, do you do anything to try to prepare yourself spiritually or emotionally for what's going to happen?

You know, I haven't really very much. And I'm just thinking, what I have done with the last two and what I'm doing right now for this one is praying a novena to St. Therese, who will be one of the patrons of this little girl. Her feast day is coming up, so I made up a little candle and picture for the baby, right in my kitchen. . . .

Could you talk about immediately after giving birth? Is that a particularly graced moment?

I have a hard time believing I'm carrying a baby until I see it. That makes faith a little hard sometimes, too, you know? It's hard to believe in a God you can't see, and yet I do. . . .

I just saw [my friend] Lucy in the hospital and all those little features on her newborn, and I was like, "She was in there! She was in there all along!" But it just looked like a little bump for so long. . . . That's quite a realization that God has done this, and wow, I had nothing much to do with it.

Immediately after her son's birth, the medical team intubated the baby to clear out any meconium he might have aspirated; alarmed, Karen called out the name of Jesus.

. . . I looked down, and I remember very clearly . . . [the baby] was just lying there on the table . . . and I was asking [the midwife], "Is he okay? Is he okay?" and apparently I called out Jesus's name. I tend to do that [in crisis] and that's a good reflex to have, probably, but I don't always know what I'm doing, and I was not swearing, I was just calling for help. And so I just remember he was blue and lifeless looking. . . . [After the intubation] he cried and pinked up and everything was fine. But shortly after that [the midwife] said, "Oh, I should've told you that's what I wanted. I didn't want him to take a breath while he was still connected to the cord, I wanted him to wait until we got him cleaned out so he didn't suck it in." And then I said, "No, it's okay, I forgive you. You did what you had to do, you don't have to make me understand everything in detail."

Right, especially when things were really time sensitive.

Right, exactly. I remember that one more clearly than the others, just being kind of prayerful in kind of a shouting way. One of my friends had a baby six weeks early, her first, and the baby was not breathing for a little while, and it was really traumatic. And she . . . was telling me, "I was shouting the Hail Mary across the room." You don't even care what people think of you, and I can just kind of picture her so consumed with concern for the child that she doesn't even care who hears. And your innermost thoughts are shouting, because we think, what else do I do? What else do I do but pray?

Well, you know, I kind of rely on the Scripture where Jesus says, "And the Holy Spirit will teach you what to say at the time of trial."[61]

And James . . . I remember my alone time with him in the room, just feeling so grateful. . . . We wanted God to be part of our decision, feeling like those [decisions to start labor] were all good decisions. We could've just gone home and said, "Oh, we'll just wait until this happens naturally," but considering that there was meconium . . . we felt like the timing [of the birth] was really divinely appointed. Or at least that we were able to discern that it would be a good time to induce labor.

Karen's story may have been affected by the reality that as she shared it with me, she was due to give birth soon, and her nervousness about the impending labor shows in her answers to these questions. What I find notable about her recounting is that she and her husband worked together, with God, to address a situation (whether to induce or not) that had no clear "right" answer. Their discernment came through prayer, asking others for prayers, and being attentive to signs. She is also very honest about her fear of pain, and the move to offer her labors to God for others is not only spiritually meaningful but also a way to "get on top" of a situation, to "give God permission" to act. She is also open to the reality that prayer isn't always "pretty"—sometimes it is shouted across the room, but that makes it no less of a prayer.

25

Kendra: "I Feel Closer to God in My Weakness"

Kendra Tierney is a married mother of seven. She lives with her family in California. This interview focuses mostly on the first time she gave birth.

My first labor we decided we wanted to labor at home. We read all the books, the natural childbirth books, and we wanted to stay home as long as possible. Once I was on board with the concepts in those books, I wanted to follow them to the letter. For example, the book said eat throughout labor [to keep up your strength], but I was nauseated and I didn't want to eat, but the book said eat so I ate, and then threw up. (*laughs*) I had to learn to listen to my body, as well.

At 12:01 AM on my due date, I went into labor with a contraction. I got up and watched a movie downstairs. Then the contractions began ramping up, and by 4 AM I wanted my husband to wake up—mostly because I needed him up! He got up and we began to walk around the apartment courtyard for a while. I tried to bathe; it felt terrible. I tried to lie down on the bed; it felt terrible. I clearly remember thinking, "I'm never doing this again!" (*laughs*) Obviously we overcame that.

The contractions were getting more and more intense, but they were farther apart than active labor is supposed to look, according to the books. *The book* said we were still in the early going, right? But they got *so* intense . . . we went in to the hospital . . . still thinking it can't get worse than this, right? The nurses' station looked at me, and they were clearly not interested. They finally checked, and I was fully dilated and ready to push! They moved me into a room and I gave birth twenty minutes later, around nine in the morning. So the labor didn't look like the book version at all!

Did you use any particular childbirth method, or did you have opinions going in about how to best give birth?

Yeah—as I was expecting my first, I researched a lot, and the Bradley Method resonated with me.

I know you have to go in with an open mind—things may not turn out the way you expect—but I was able to use that method successfully. That worked well for us. We had natural childbirths, all seven.

We went to the hospital each time. I'd be happy to do home birth but I think that is something everyone needs to be on board with, and my husband is much more comfortable with a hospital birth. We labor as long as we can at home. Honestly, we've been doing this so long we are going to give birth the way we want to, whether at home or in a hospital. We know how to do this, and are not intimidated by hospital protocols at this point. It works out fine.

Did you engage in any spiritual practices prior to birth? Can you describe them?

That's evolved for me. I see birth now as an opportunity for suffering that could be offered up. I viewed it as a physical challenge in the beginning—you know, something to accomplish, like a marathon. But I didn't see it as a way to offer my physical sufferings to God for others. Around my third one, I saw it as a way to offer my sufferings. . . . And we always pray for the baby.

The suffering in childbirth is such a perfect opportunity: it's relatively short (in duration), you know it has an end—it's not like an illness, not a lifetime of suffering. It's intense suffering, and for a good reason. Maybe if I have a serious illness, the birth experience will be good preparation for handling that, but I don't know.

I'm a runner, so I've experienced pain to some extent. I know the reality of intensity in pursuit of a goal, a race, a time—so maybe I already had good preparation for viewing suffering in pursuit of a goal as something doable, and worth doing.

Have your births been painful?

They have been painful but manageable. I have had labors from nine hours long to one and a half hours [with the exception of one that was two days] . . . but you get breaks in labor, too. Manageable seems to be the right word.

I offered to take prayer intentions at my last birth. I took them to the hospital. And at one point, we were walking around through the contractions, and I thought, wait, this isn't hard enough! Oh no! But things got challenging at the end. There is always some point of a birth that is very challenging.

Did you engage in any spiritual practices during your birth?

Taking the prayer intentions is the main thing; I've done that for my last three children. And they [the people who give her intentions to offer] pray for me. Their prayers increase my ability to focus; I am sure of it. We always have holy water with us, in case of an emergency baptism, but we have not needed it.

I definitely turn inward during childbirth. I don't have the energy to expend on other people, to focus on external objects, like a crucifix or holy card, to listen to music. It's very inward, my attention is there.

In retrospect, where was God in your birthing process? Was there a place where you sensed the presence of the Holy Spirit? Or Mary?

I think I feel closer to God in my weakness. Pregnancy and childbirth is the most vulnerable I've ever felt. I'm mostly naked, surrounded by strangers, in intense physical pain, and doing something that has at least a chance of killing me or someone I love. That's a lot to handle by myself. Too much. In that situation, it feels easier to know I *must* rely on others, on my husband and my doctor, and on God.

To me, the most notable element in Kendra's lovely story is recognizing that the weakness that one feels in childbirth can help one realize one's absolute dependence on God in a way that doesn't happen in everyday life. Our culture often ridicules weakness, but for Christians it can be seen as a path to God. The notable other piece is the turning inward that is so much a part of active labor. Some midwives would say you are listening to your body—and at some level, you are—but that move to inwardness can also be a sign of listening for God. Something to consider. . . .

26

Regina: "After the C-Sections, I See the Hand of God in All Things"

Regina Hiney is a married mother of six who lives in Virginia. All of her births have been by Cesarean section.

I had six C-sections. My first "to term" pregnancy—I had a second trimester miscarriage—was a C-section because my son was 10.4 pounds and fully breach. My doctor tried turning him but his head was lodged somewhere under my rib cage. When it looked like I was developing preeclampsia (a spike in blood pressure, swelling, and headache) the doctor made the decision to go ahead and do the C-section.

When I was pregnant with my second child we did try for a VBAC [vaginal birth after Cesarean]. It was a planned birth: pitocin, hooked up to machines. And they took the baby a week early [because] I was having another big baby (she was my smallest at 8 pounds, 13 ounces).

After sixteen hours, labor "failed to progress," and it was discovered that the baby (Katherine) was in distress with the umbilical cord around her neck—twice. We wound up having an emergency C-section. There was disappointment. I remember thinking that if maybe I had let nature take its natural course—not gone early, not had the pitocin, no machines . . . I think maybe things would have gone differently. But maybe then the cord could have gotten around Katherine's neck and things could have gone badly. After two C-sections, the rest were just planned C-sections. So, I tend to see the hand of God in all things.

Did you engage in any spiritual practices directed toward the birth prior to this birth? Can you describe them?

I am Catholic but my husband is not. So, I prepared by going to Confession. Jason and I will pray together. My Bible study friends pray for me and folks from both my church and Jason's church prayed for us.

Where was God in your birthing process? Was there a place where you sensed the presence of the Holy Spirit? Or Mary?

One neat story as I was having my fifth C-section [happened when] Jason wasn't in the room yet—he had to get prepped.

The nurses always are floored when they hear that I am not getting my tubes tied "while the doctor is in there anyway." Victoria is only fifteen months younger than my daughter Mary and it was a difficult pregnancy. And I was feeling *tremendous* pressure to have my tubes tied. I was scared. I was tired. I was sick. I had been pregnant and nursing for ten years and I *wanted* to be done. But I also knew what the Church taught. And I was tempted to just go ahead and have the old tubes tied . . . so tempted.

I prayed. It was literally a split-second decision. My husband, not being Catholic, would have supported my decision. I really wanted to be done. . . .

The husband of one of my best friends, a devout Catholic, was my anesthetist. And they asked if I wanted my tubes tied. And I will never forget as he was checking all the equipment . . . he looked over and said, "Tubes tied? Are you kidding me? Have you seen this woman's kids? She makes beautiful children! The world cannot be denied more Hineys!"

It was just a simple humorous statement. But it was enough. I did not have my tubes tied. Four years later, I had my third son and sixth child. And such a blessing.

Was it disappointing to have a scheduled C-section? Or a relief? Or in between?

Mostly I know how my body now reacts to the meds, to the surgery, and to the shock. I know I have to move my legs and walk. I don't let myself get stiff. I walk as soon as I can out of recovery. Hurts like crazy at first, but it pays off the next day. I know my body so I have found that my recovery from C-sections is much easier with each one. And since I don't know any other way to give birth—better the devil you know than the devil you don't.

These last three stories are about women who gave birth through Cesarean section. The key to seeing the sign of birth in this situation is recognizing the hand of God in the process that determines that a C-section is in the best interest of the mother and baby; signs may also be spotted in the operating room. Regina's story speaks to that, and the peace she has around the C-sections also witnesses to her openness to God's work through this way of birth. For the record, women who have a planned C-section can certainly expect to be asked about whether they want an elective tubal ligation: being prepared with an answer would be wise. (Although the way God spoke through her friend in the operating room in her story is wonderful!)

27

Jennifer: "Mary Became My Lifeline"

Jennifer D. is a married mother of four children (three biological and one adopted). She and her husband are in the process of adopting two more children, blood siblings. She also had two Cesarean sections, although she was less sanguine about it than Regina (the mother in the previous story). She lives in rural Illinois.

My last birth—Daniel Anthony—was a scheduled C-section. [His older sister] Anna was born via emergency C-section (general anesthesia), and at the time she was born, my ob-gyn stood at my bedside and *assured* me that this in no way meant that I would never have another vaginal birth, that his VBAC [vaginal birth after Cesarean] rate was high, etc.

By the time I met him in his office [before Daniel's birth], he was singing a different tune. Statistics and risks and blah, blah, blah—I was basically bullied into having another section, told that I would absolutely not be allowed to VBAC at any of the hospitals where he had privileges, that I would be putting myself and my baby at risk, etc. I asked a lot of questions, I did my research, and, honestly, it was the high cost of medical malpractice in Illinois that drove all of this—doctors who performed VBACs were risking losing coverage and hospitals simply weren't allowing it.

I was horribly disappointed, but torn. We live in the boonies; to find a hospital or birthing center that would accommodate my desire to VBAC, I would have had to travel forty-plus minutes, in labor, to deliver. And with two little ones at home, that didn't make sense.

I pushed the date of the scheduled section out as far as I could—delivering just four days before Daniel's due date—in the hopes that I would go into labor on my own (I never have) and arrive at the hospital so far into labor that they would have no choice but to deliver me. No such luck. We arrived in the wee hours for my intake, walked to the OR carrying my catheter bag (*really*?), and Daniel was born—after I was given a spinal tap—at 7:56 AM.

I should add that anyone doing anything to my spine freaks me out—I have had a bad back since my early twenties. I begged for Michael to be allowed to be with me for the spinal tap and was denied even that. Thank goodness I did have an amazing nurse and an amazing anesthesiologist. I begged for the sheet to be left down. My arms were strapped—I was basically crucified there on the operating table, which couldn't have been wider than a yardstick—and it was freezing cold in that room. I wanted to watch. I assured them I was not grossed out. I wanted to see Daniel born. Nope. They even assumed we knew the baby's gender—we didn't—and we *had to ask* them to tell us boy or girl. Lots of pulling and tugging—no pain at all—it all went pretty fast.

Back in recovery, my blood pressure would not rebound—I typically have low blood pressure—and they tilted my bed to elevate my feet, then it got stuck that way and they had to call maintenance in to work on the bed in which I was recovering.

Was it disappointing to have a scheduled C-section? Or a relief? Or in between?

I was annoyed to have to recover from what I saw as unnecessary surgery with three little ones at home. It was not the birth experience I hoped for or dreamed of, but I was not disappointed. I was healthy, Daniel was healthy—hard to argue with that outcome—but I know, in my gut, that's not how childbirth is supposed to go. If I were to become pregnant today, I would VBAC regardless of distance . . . I'm no risk at all.

Do you have opinions going in about how to best give birth?

Yes. Michael and I took the Bradley childbirth classes prior to Rebecca's birth. She was born twenty hours after my membranes were broken. She was a week late and we went in for an induction, but I asked to be allowed to try to labor before they gave me pitocin—the only medication I had was lidocaine for an episiotomy the doctor chose to perform because I was tearing up instead of down.

Did you engage in any spiritual practices directed toward the birth prior to this birth? Can you describe them?

When I was pregnant with Anna, our priest and deacon presented us with a blessed St. Gabriel medal which I wore until after she was born. When I learned I was pregnant with Daniel (on a Sunday afternoon), I put on my medal again. At Mass the following Sunday, I was lector. In the sacristy, I met Deacon Bob. He *immediately* noticed my medal, gasped, came close and asked if it meant what he thought it meant. And then he asked permission and blessed my babe. And every Sunday that I received Holy Communion from him, he blessed my babe. He was to baptize Daniel, but he died suddenly that January, before Daniel was born.

Did you engage in any spiritual practices during your birth?

No. Well, I'm sure I had people praying for me. I know I did. But not beyond that.

Where was God in your birthing process? Was there a place where you sensed the presence of the Holy Spirit? Or Mary?

When I found out I was pregnant with Daniel, I cried for two days. I have come to refer to Daniel as the "best present we never asked for." Michael and I were not taught—*not even in marriage preparation*—about the Church's stand on birth control. Not once ever—except that my mother would sometimes make disparaging remarks about it. When we were married—before and after Rebecca's birth—we used birth control. It took us one glance to become pregnant with Rebecca. It took a year of charting and worrying and trying to become pregnant with Anna.

After Anna's birth, I refused to take the Pill and I had a bad allergic reaction to spermicide. At one point I recall asking Deacon Bob why couples who had children couldn't decide "they were done." He gently (and kind of embarrassingly) guided me to an NFP couple in our parish. I became convicted long, long before Michael, and he respectfully went along with my belief that this was true Church teaching and we needed to follow it. Daniel, though the charts would suggest he shouldn't be here, was conceived while we were using NFP. We still weren't at the point of being open and accepting that God's will in this matter was wiser than ours.

About a week after I learned I was pregnant with Daniel, the Christmas carol "Gabriel's Message" (by Sting) popped into my head—*in September*—and I was bowled over by Mary's acceptance of this child God asked her to carry. In that moment, Mary became my lifeline, my beacon, my role model; my favorite verse since then has been, if I'm asked to give one, Luke 1:38.

Luke 1:38 reads: "'Here am I, the servant of the Lord; let it be with me according to your word.' Then the angel departed from her."

Anything you want to add?

Want one more crazy story? When Daniel was about three years old, someone asked him if he had any brothers or sisters. He said he had two sisters. The questioner said, "No brothers?" And Daniel said, "Not yet!" Some weeks later, Daniel said he wanted a brother, "and not a baby. I want a brother who can talk to me and play with me." After we adopted Joshua, who is five days shy of being nine months older than Daniel, we realized that Daniel was conceived about a week or two after Joshua was born. We never would have sought specifically a child of Joshua's age—and specifically a boy—if not for Daniel being here. We meant to adopt a younger brother, but God made sure [we] found Joshua [through Daniel's desire].

Jennifer had at least one C-section she did not want, for reasons that she felt were not valid. I would suggest that women with similar stories seek a way of healing and forgiveness (which she may well have done, since she is at peace with what happened). What this story does well is move beyond the circumstances of the birth and see the child's conception and life as a part of God's larger plan for their family, and even for a little boy they were destined to adopt years later.

28

Nora: "I Kept Thinking, 'This is My Body, Given Up for You'"

Nora (another requested pseudonym) is a married mother of three children and lives in Texas. All three of her children were born by Cesarean section.

My first Cesarean section came at the end of a failed induction, after I'd been laboring for close to twenty-four hours. I was fifteen days past my due date and finally agreed to let my doctor perform an induction, still hopeful that this could result in a low-intervention birth. We hired our Bradley Method instructor as our doula and she was with us for most of the induction. When, after hours of active labor, I was still barely dilated, we agreed that a C-section was the only option. Our doula said that we were her first C-section in over two hundred births, but she also agreed that this was definitely the way to go.

I remember being very overwrought and thanking the entire medical team, giving thanks that I lived somewhere with modern medical care, saying something like, "I could just be *dying* somewhere in a *field. . . .*"

I also was very conscious of feeling "crucified" for the surgery itself because it required strapping my arms down to the table. I am terrified of needles. I kept thinking, *"This is my body, given up for you."* It was definitely an abandonment of all of the hopes I had brought to the birth, and a surrender.

I had a difficult recovery and my son was in the NICU [neonatal intensive care unit], just for a few days, to get his breathing straightened out. My father was in the end stages of cancer at the time and my mom was not able to come out to assist us right away. I felt very doubtful about my own abilities as a mother and kept second-guessing the decisions we had made along the way: resisting my doctor's suggestion that we induce a few weeks earlier, asserting our preferences for an unmedicated birth and ending up with the opposite. We did have tremendously supportive friends and family.

My second time around, I hoped for a VBAC [vaginal birth after Cesarean] because we knew we wanted a large family and I didn't want to keep having C-sections. My daughter was breech at the final ultrasound they performed a few days before the surgery, and neither my doctor nor I wished to attempt a VBAC in those circumstances. She flipped her little self right back around by the day of the surgery, but we didn't want to fight with my doctor. I also knew that a scheduled C-section would be much less physically draining than having the surgery at the end of a long, painful labor.

The surgery went well, but my daughter was gravely ill at birth with a lung defect. She was baptized the day after she was born, and had to be flown via helicopter to a different hospital a couple of hours away soon afterward. I was very, very aware of all of the prayers of my family and friends. I associate the mystery of the Visitation with this birth experience, because Elizabeth was Mary's family as well as her friend, and she provided her with such encouragement. I said the rosary at my daughter's bedside. My father had died a couple of years beforehand and I had reached the point in life where you stop thinking God is going to protect you from anything really bad happening, so it was in some ways a crisis of faith; but, at the same time, I felt tremendous peace and that I was not alone.

My third C-section was also scheduled, and my younger son was also in the NICU, but with a less serious issue than with my daughter. We had some of the same staff at the NICU for his birth as for my daughter's, and for the most part they were absolutely wonderful. I did have one nurse comment along the lines of, "I'm amazed you had another one after what you went through last time," and it made me feel really ashamed to think that other people might be judging us to be foolhardy about the risks of having another child.

Was it disappointing to have scheduled C-sections? Or a relief? Or in between?

Disappointing but also something I felt was the best possible option given the circumstances. I still have a lot of fear and guilt attached to my original C-section and have to remind myself that it's not my fault that each child ended up in the NICU. (They all are very healthy today, with active, some might say overused—ha-ha!—lungs.) It's hard not to retrace my steps and wonder if I might have more children today if I had followed more of my doctor's advice the first time and could have avoided a C-section and the attendant "drama."

Did you have opinions going in about how to best give birth?

Yes, but I also based many of those opinions on fear of needles. I was hopeful that I could have an unmedicated birth but didn't really like being "anti–medical establishment."

Did you engage in any spiritual practices during your birth?

Asking people to pray for me, yes, and doing a lot of deep

breaths and repetitive prayer because I find the process of being prepped for surgery to be, frankly, terrifying.

In retrospect, where was God in your birthing process? Was there a place where you sensed the presence of the Holy Spirit? Or Mary?

I think I kind of answered that above. . . . I don't really like to point to specific things and say, "God was definitely doing this particular thing in my life." I would say I definitely associate these experiences with surrender and with knowing I am not alone, and that my baby is loved even more deeply than I myself am capable of. I also grew in devotion to Mary specifically with the birth of my daughter.

Is there anything else you would like to add?

I don't remember who it was I talked to at the time, but I remember this friend specifically saying that it was okay to grieve over aspects of my first birth experience, and that it didn't mean I was just being selfish and not appreciating the gift of my newborn son.

This whole area of family size, birthing, risky birthing, etc., is a very painful one for me. I kind of hate the whole "being Catholic means you need to be ready to discuss fertility with strangers at any time" thing.

(Thus we ask—why did I answer the questions? Heh.)

I am not sure why Nora answered these questions, but I am glad she overcame her ambivalence and did so. One of the pieces that struck me most in this account of her three C-section births is that she said that the prominent spiritual sense was that she was not alone. These were certainly high-risk births and the way the children were born may have been of much less concern than their health; she was certainly grateful that she and her children could take advantage of the Cesarean. But importantly, she felt she was not alone, that God was present to her in the operating room (fear and terror not withstanding) and in the NICU, praying the rosary with and for her child. If this is not openness to God and yielding to the work of the Holy Spirit, I don't know what is.

Notes

1. Margaret Guenther, *Holy Listening: The Art of Spiritual Direction* (Cambridge, MA: Cowley Publications, 1992), 85.

2. Kathy Pesta, September 25, 2009 (12:37 p.m.), comment on Susan Windley-Daoust, "A Fiery Gift," *America*, October 5, 2009, http://americamagazine.org/issue/709/article/fiery-gift.

3. Sandy Smith, September 28, 2009 (10:02 a.m.), comment on Windley-Daoust, "A Fiery Gift," http://americamagazine.org/issue/709/article/fiery-gift.

4. Many people, including Catholics, don't think about this unity of body and soul accurately, and tend to emphasize one aspect of the human being over the other. Be careful! We would be better served by using terms like "embodied soul," "ensouled body," or "soul-body composite." We are not angels—all spirit. We are not animals, either. Humanity is unique in that we are created body and soul, integrated together into a whole. The influence of soul on body and body on soul is real.

5. Christopher West is the best known popularizer of the Theology of the Body audiences, and his *Theology of the Body for Beginners* is a place to start for those who are completely new to the school of thought, as it is written to people who are not theologians. Another text of his that I appreciate even more is *Fill These Hearts*, which is also readable and focuses more on what it means to be human rather than the nature of sexuality and marriage. If you have more theological background, you may wish to look at Mary Shivanandan's *Crossing the Threshold of Love*, or the audiences of Pope St. John Paul II themselves, which include a fine academic introduction by Michael Waldstein. Christopher West, *Theology of the Body for Beginners: A Basic Introduction to Pope John Paul II's Sexual Revolution* (West Chester, PA: Ascension Press, 2004); Christopher West, *Fill These Hearts: God, Sex, and the Universal Longing* (New York: Image, 2012); Mary Shivanandan, *Crossing the Threshold of Love: A New Vision of Marriage* (Washington, DC: Catholic University

of America Press, 1999); John Paul II, and Michael Waldstein ed., *Man and Woman He Created Them: A Theology of the Body* (Boston, MA: Pauline Books & Media, 2006).

6. For those interested in deeper reading on the Theology of the Body, John Paul II most directly addresses the effect of original sin on perception in *Man and Woman He Created Them*, §26. I also address the fallenness of our sight in chapter 1 of my earlier work, *Theology of the Body, Extended: The Spiritual Signs of Birth, Impairment, and Dying* (Hobe Sound, FL: Lectio Publishing, 2014).

7. She had begun her twelve-hour shift by introducing herself, and after asking me where I worked (I worked for a Catholic university teaching theology), responded that she had worked for Planned Parenthood before taking this job. My husband said after the birth, and still says now, that explains a lot. She saw birth as a product and was inured to the pain of women. Unfortunately, I think he was right. It is also possible, due to my job title, she saw me as an enemy from the time we met.

8. See John 8:44: "…When [the Devil] lies, he speaks according to his own nature, for he is a liar and the father of lies." Unless otherwise noted, all Biblical quotations are from the New Revised Standard Version, Catholic Edition, translation.

9. A doula is a person, usually a woman, with training in helping women give birth naturally, but doulas deliberately work alongside medical professionals, and see their role as one of primary attention on the process of labor and the well-being of the mother while in labor. They often serve as a patient advocate in a hospital setting, and help the laboring woman in a more focused and present way than typical hospital protocols allow of hospital staff. Some hospitals are not welcoming of doulas, but many are, especially since there are many studies that show the presence of a doula within a labor decreases the need for medical interventions dramatically.

10. A compound presentation means that a limb and the baby's head are coming out together (for example, hand next to head) rather than the baby's limbs resting in the classic fetal position.

11. William Sears, M.D., and Martha Sears, R.N. *The Birth Book: Everything You Need to Know to Have a Safe and Satisfying Birth*

(Boston: Little, Brown and Co., 1994). The book is slightly dated but the principles are still very sound.

12. Vividly remembered from a lecture I heard when I was an undergraduate at Mary Washington College (now University of Mary Washington) in Fredericksburg, VA. The lecturer was a college professor and United Church of Christ minister named David Cain. This quotation is presented in his voice.

13. John Paul II, *Man and Woman He Created Them*, §17. "So she finds herself again in the very fact of giving herself 'through a sincere gift of herself,' (cf. *Gaudium et Spes* §24), when she is accepted in the way in which the Creator wished her to be, that is, 'for her own sake,' through her humanity and femininity."

14. George Weigel, *Witness to Hope: The Biography of Pope John Paul II: 1920–2005* (New York: Harper Perennial, 2005), 343.

15. John Paul II, *Man and Woman He Created Them*, §21:2.

16. John Paul II, *Man and Woman He Created Them*, §21:6.

17. John Paul II, *Man and Woman He Created Them*, §21:2.

18. John Paul II, *Man and Woman He Created Them*, Waldstein introduction, 105.

19. Pastoral Constitution on the Church in the Modern World, *Gaudium et Spes,* Promulgated by His Holiness, Pope Paul VI, On December 7, 1965, §24, http://www.vatican.va/archive/hist_councils/ii_vatican_council/documents/vat-ii_cons_19651207_gaudium-et-spes_en.html. This line was one of John Paul II's favorite lines from the Second Vatican II, and he was on the committee that created this pastoral constitution.

20. This rendition comes from David Fleming's modern reading of the Spiritual Exercises: David L. Fleming S.J., *Draw Me into Your Friendship: The Spiritual Exercises: A Literal Translation & a Contemporary Reading* (St. Louis, MO: Institute of Jesuit Sources, 1996), 27.

21. Henri J. M. Nouwen, *With Open Hands* (Notre Dame, IN: Ave Maria Press, 1972), 154.

22. Women aren't receptacles, and men aren't generators; the relationship is a great deal more nuanced than that, and identifying either gender with one gift misunderstands the wholeness of each person.

23. Augustine, *On the Trinity*, XV.19.36, quoted in Raniero Cantalamessa, *Come, Creator Spirit: Meditations on the* Veni Creator (Collegeville, MN: Liturgical Press, 2003), 80.

24. 1 Corinthians 6:19.

25. Cantalamessa, *Come, Creator Spirit*, 88-93.

26. I address the definitions of both *behold* and *gaze* more thoroughly through Scripture and philosophy in my book *Theology of the Body, Extended*, beginning at pp. 16–17.

27. The one exception was another birth narrative, the birth of Jabez (1 Chronicles 4:9). Interestingly, John Paul II wrote extensively on the concept of work versus toil in what is one of his most creative encyclicals, *Laborem Exercens* (see especially §27). But he does not tackle the issue of toil as an aspect of childbirth (he does speak of the toil of a mother rearing a family, but childbirth is never mentioned as part of that). Basically, John Paul II argues we consider work as part of the calling of what it means to be a thriving human being, and toil as the difficulty of work after the Fall. There can be a blessing buried within some natural toil, but the destructive difficulty of it is part of the fallen condition.

28. The Septuagint is a Greek translation of the Hebrew Scriptures, legendarily created by seventy rabbis, dating about 200 BC. Sometimes it is abbreviated LXX (for the seventy).

29. Biblical scholar Carol Meyers argues persuasively that *eseb* does not refer to physical pain but to emotional challenge. Her preferred translation of the word is "travail." Carol Meyers, *Discovering Eve: Ancient Israelite Women in Context* (New York: Oxford University Press, 1988), 106–8.

30. Helen Wessel, *Natural Childbirth and the Christian Family* (New York: Harper and Row, 1963), 57–59.

31. "An Act of Trust," available at http://archive.austindiocese.org/dept/vocations/prayers.php.

32. This is suggested by the extracanonical *Protoevangelium of James*, written in the early second century, and the legend is assumed by most of the early Church. There is a very helpful discussion of it in the unusually winsome book *Mary: A Catholic-Evangelical Debate*, in the fourth chapter on the perpetual virginity of Mary. Dwight Longenecker and David Gustafson, *Mary: A Catholic-Evangelical Debate* (Grand Rapids, MI: Brazos Press, 2003), 63–78.

33. John Paul II, *Crossing the Threshold of Hope* (New York: Alfred A. Knopf, 1995), 36.

34. Kara McIntee, interview with author, June 11, 2014.

35. Sherry Antonetti, interview with author, June 11, 2014.

36. This first line of Psalm 16 is from the New American Bible Revised Edition.

37. This question is posed in Adrian Reimers's "Human Suffering and John Paul II's Theology of the Body," *Nova et Vetera* 2(2) (Fall 2004): 445–60.

38. *Birth* also has an etymological root in the word *wave*: "*bara*," the root, is Old Norse for "wave, billow, or bore." Vangie Bergum, "Birthing Pain," *Phenomenology Online*, accessed October 12, 2012, http://www.phenomenologyonline.com/sources/textorium/bergum-vangie-birthing-pain/.

39. Emilie Griffin, *Clinging: The Experience of Prayer* (San Francisco: Harper and Row, 1984), 20.

40. *Catechism of the Catholic Church*, 2nd ed. (Washington, D.C: United States Catholic Conference, 2011) (digital edition), #692, reprinted at: http://www.vatican.va/archive/ccc_css/archive/catechism/p1s2c3a8.htm.

41. Ellen D. Hodnett, Simon Gates, G. Justus Hofmeyr, and Carol Sakala, "Continuous support for women during childbirth," Cochrane Database of Systematic Reviews, 10 (2012): Art. No.: CD003766, DOI: 10.1002/14651858.CD003766.pub4, available at http://onlinelibrary.wiley.com/doi/10.1002/14651858 .CD003766.pub4/abstract.

42. De Caussade, *The Joy of Full Surrender*, trans. Hal M. Helm (Brewster, MA: Paraclete Press, 1986), 125–26.

43. Catechism §2672 says the Holy Spirit is "the interior Master of Christian prayer," and the instigator of prayer as the work of the Holy Spirit in a person is witnessed at Romans 8:26 above, as well as Ephesians 6:18, and Luke 11:13. *Catechism of the Catholic Church*, 2nd ed. (Washington, D.C: United States Catholic Conference, 2011) (digital edition), #2672, reprinted at: http://www.vatican.va/archive/ccc_css/archive/catechism/p4s1c2a2.htm.

44. http://catholicism.about.com/od/prayers/qt/Lorica_Patrick.htm.

45. This is with the obvious exception of my first birth, where pushing never really got started. Frankly, even the birth that had a compound presentation didn't feel *too* bad to me.

46. In some Eastern cultures, the birthing of the placenta is important: the placenta may be saved and planted under a tree, and, in some cultures, ritually consumed (in part). There is really no Western tradition of anything like this.

47. Pope John Paul II, *Love & Responsibility*, rev. ed. (New York: Farrar, Straus & Giroux, Inc., 1981), 201.

48. Ibid., 207.

49. Fleming, Draw Me Into Your Friendship, 27.

50. Centers for Disease Control and Prevention, FastStats: Infertility, http://www.cdc.gov/nchs/fastats/infertility.htm (accessed December 12, 2015).

51. Rebecca Frech, "Breaking the Façade," *Shoved to Them*, March

16, 2014, available at http://www.patheos.com/blogs/rebecca-frech/2014/03/breaking-the-facade.html.

52. American Pregnancy Association, "Miscarriage," accessed December 13, 2015, available at http://americanpregnancy.org/pregnancycomplications/miscarriage.html.

53. Blessing of Parents After a Miscarriage or Stillbirth, reprinted at: http://www.usccb.org/prayer-and-worship/bereavement-and-funerals/blessing-of-parents-after-a-miscarriage-or-stillbirth.cfm. *Book of Blessings*, © 1988, United States Conference of Catholic Bishops, Washington, DC.

54. National Conference of Catholic Bishops, *Order of Christian Funerals* (Totowa, NJ: Catholic Book Publishing Co., 1989).

55. *Catechism of the Catholic Church*, #1261, reprinted at http://www.vatican.va/archive/ccc_css/archive/catechism/p2s2c1a1.htm.

56. Dr. William and Martha Sears have a good chapter on how to "humanize" a high-tech birth in *The Birth Book*, chap. 13.

57. Janice Croze, "Surviving Postpartum Depression," *Guideposts*, https://www.guideposts.org/surviving-postpartum-depression?nopaging=1.

58. Centers for Disease Control and Prevention, http://www.cdc.gov/reproductivehealth/depression/ (accessed December 31, 2015).

59. Luke 18:38.

60. Leah lives in Canada, and using laughing gas as an aid to birth is not uncommon there. This is not typical in the United States.

61. Paraphrase of Luke 12:12.

Acknowledgments

I thank many women for their graciousness is consenting to interviews regarding their birth experiences, some of whom were fine with a full-name acknowledgment, others with a first name, and others with a pseudonym for privacy: Kara McIntee, Sherry Antonetti, Leann Putz, Laura L., Carla, Jennifer Wendt, Christie Martin, Jaye, Karen, Regina Hiney, Jennifer D., Nora, and Kendra Tierney. These generous women shared their birth stories with me in the summer and fall of 2014, and many are found in the stories in Part Four, in many chapter epigraphs, and in some of the suggestions for prayerful reflection.

I also thank many women for reading sections of the manuscript for conversation and critique: Mary Maselko, Jaye, Karee Santos, Maggie Geene, and Hannah Sumpter. There was also a group of forty women who graciously joined a "Christian Reflections on Childbirth" private group on Facebook to chat about the spiritual elements of all sorts of birth situations; those conversations were invaluable.

And last but definitely not least, I have to acknowledge my husband. If he had not been on board to join me in the adventure and challenge that is giving birth, I don't know if I ever would have had the imaginative spark to tackle this book.

Thank you all for your support, for sharing stories, and for sharing the love of our gracious God.